C000015647

'Punchy, well written and forensic in its analysis. Exposes how attacks on rail workers' terms and conditions have been at the heart of privatisation – and how passengers and taxpayers have also been fleeced by shareholders and bosses.'

**Frances O'Grady, General Secretary,
Trades Union Congress**

'A clear, precise and accessible glide through the disastrous history of British privatised rail and a passionate case for why we need the railways now more than ever, *Derailed* is an InterCity125 in a discourse dominated by Pacers and Pendolinos.'

**Owen Hatherley, culture editor of *Tribune* and
author of *Modern Buildings in Britain***

'Tom Haines-Doran provides an excellent summary of the wrongs of rail privatisation, but that's the easy bit. The best sections of the book are those attempting to provide ideas for sorting out the mess and giving the railways the focus they need to survive at a time of concerns about climate change and inequality.'

Christian Wolmar, author of *British Rail: A New History*

'*Derailed* is a fascinating and readable guide to the state of the UK's railways, which shows exactly what needs to be done to build a rail network that works for public good rather than private profit.'

Grace Blakeley, author of *The Corona Crash*

'*Derailed* is a brilliant, revelatory book. Deeply researched, lucidly written and humane, it explains the chronic failure of corner-cutting, under-funding and privatisation in Britain's railways – and more importantly, what we can do about it. I commend this book to anyone who has ever wondered why things don't work properly in this country, and wants to know how to fix it.'

Richard Seymour, author of *The Twittering Machine*

'*Derailed* is, in short, an indispensable read for anyone with even a passing interest in the railways, either as a passenger or member of staff. I hope that both unions and passengers' groups take notice of it. It can inform the movement well for the next stages of the struggle to get the public-transport system we so urgently need.'

Kevin Crane, *Counterfire*

Derailed

Manchester University Press

Derailed

How to fix Britain's broken railways

Tom Haines-Doran

MANCHESTER UNIVERSITY PRESS

The right of Tom Haines-Doran to be identified as the author of this work
has been asserted by them in accordance with the Copyright, Designs and
Patents Act 1988.

Published by Manchester University Press
Oxford Road, Manchester M13 9PL

www.manchesteruniversitypress.co.uk

British Library Cataloguing-in-Publication Data
A catalogue record for this book is available from the British Library

ISBN 978 1 5261 6405 6 paperback

First published 2022

Typeset
by Cheshire Typesetting Ltd, Cuddington, Cheshire
Printed in Great Britain
by CPI Group (UK) Ltd, Croydon, CR0 4YY

For Max

Happy travels

Contents

List of figures

Acknowledgements

Thank you to commissioning editor Tom Dark, and series editors Julie Froud and Karel Williams, for their incredible support and insight in helping me get this book together. They promised me a 'hands-on' approach, which is exactly what I got, and that has made for a much better book.

This book represents a culmination of several years' work researching the political economy of railways in Britain. That journey began as a master's project, under the supervision of Ian Bruff at the University of Manchester. Without his encouragement, I probably would not have pursued, or have the ability to pursue, a career in academic research. A huge amount of gratitude must also go to Ben Fine at SOAS, whose brilliance as a PhD supervisor and academic is legendary. I have been very lucky indeed to have had them as mentors. This book is a very different (little) beast compared with my academic dissertations, but its arguments would have been far weaker without the background theoretical and research work they involved.

Other people in the academic and transport worlds worthy of special thanks include Steve Rolf, Andy Brown, Julia Steinberger, Greg Marsden, Kate Bayliss, Jefim Vogel, Ersilia Verlinghieri,

Giulio Mattioli and Jonathan Bray. Thanks also to Christian Wolmar and Jean Shaoul for their help at various points.

Thanks to those who I have worked with as I have tried to involve myself in transport campaigning while writing this book, not least rail workers Clayton and Conor, Emily Yates from the Association of British Commuters and activists in Streets for People Levenshulme and Burnage.

Finally, thank you to friends and family for their support, especially Emma Chorlton.

Introduction

The 18:57 from London Euston

A delayed train: it's one of the few occasions that strangers talk to each other in Britain, at least while sober. Nothing can unite young and old, rich and poor like a good old moan about the state of the railways.

It was a wet Wednesday evening in March 2019. I was riding the 18:57 from London Euston to Manchester Piccadilly. The train was packed with commuters, day trippers and crying babies. The air was close, and condensation fogged the windows. Things had gone well until just after Milton Keynes, when we had become inexplicably stuck somewhere in the Northamptonshire countryside.

Ironically, I was on my way home from a conference where I had presented some of my research on the economics of rail privatisation. The presentation had gone OK – I managed to get through the PowerPoint slides and there were some incisive questions, which I thought I'd handled fairly well. But I was tired, and – albeit delayed – the ride home to Manchester was a chance to switch off from the stresses of academia and get stuck into that novel I never seemed to have time to read.

'And what about you mate? What do you do?'

Looking up from the page, I saw that the middle-aged man sitting directly opposite me was trying to get me involved in the conversation that had sprung up among the three other occupants of our table of four. It had started with complaining about the delay, and speculation over the causes, before migrating to reasons for travelling and introductions. Sam was a physiotherapist from south London who was travelling to Stockport for an appointment the next morning; Alisha was an account manager from Bolton on her way home from a meeting; and Ruth was an undergraduate at the University of Salford, where she was returning after seeing some friends. I was in no mood to engage. But when you're stuck on a train with strangers, there's nowhere to hide.

When I told them that I had been researching the politics and economics of railways for many years, their eyes lit up. I was subjected to a barrage of questions about why the railways were in such a state of disarray. Who was to blame? What could be done? I started to get into it. Over the course of the journey I managed to offload much of my accumulated knowledge and opinions, which have formed over years of academic research, professional involvement and activism related to transport. It helped pass the time on a journey which, thanks to repeated delays, was to become epic.

But the experience left me troubled. As much as I'd enjoyed fielding the questions, they made me realise that what I had been researching was not necessarily what people wanted to know. What is the point of academic study unless it is useful to the real-world problems people face? Because the questions they asked were not the ones I had focussed on in my studies, I wasn't satisfied with the answers I gave.

So I told Sam, Alisha and Ruth that I would write them a book, and here it is. This is for them and for the millions of people who rely on Britain's railways.

How did we get here?

This book will address the main concerns passengers have about Britain's beleaguered railway system. In Chapter 1: why don't the trains run on time? In Chapter 2: why are fares so high? In Chapter 3: why are there so many strikes? In Chapter 4: how can we hold those in charge to account? In Chapter 5: what are the prospects for fixing the system?

The answers provided refer to how the railways have developed since the privatisation of British Railways in the mid-1990s. But before we move to the answers, it's a good idea to sketch out how the modern railway system developed in Britain, because it's only with that history in mind that we can understand how we got to privatisation and the problems it would cause.

Britain was the first country in the world to develop passenger rail services. The first intercity passenger railway, and the first that would be recognisable to modern rail passengers – with station platforms and scheduled services – was the Liverpool and Manchester Railway, opened in 1830. The success of the Liverpool and Manchester prompted a massive boom in railway investment and construction, unhindered by governments which favoured free market development and little regulation. Railways competed with each other for business, often building duplicate infrastructure to serve given flows or destinations. This resulted in a fragmented patchwork of short lines, making it difficult to convey goods or passengers on longer, 'through' journeys. Although many railways provided passenger services, their primary purpose was to serve Britain's heavy extractive industries, such as coal, iron and steel ore.

The boom quickly became a bubble. In a period now known as 'railway mania', which lasted until 1846, 272 Acts of Parliament were passed to set up and construct new railways. Some of the routes established in this period remained in operation for many years (and some to this day), but a significant proportion of the projects proved unviable, and an economically destructive crash was the inevitable result.

There followed a period of consolidation, during which the larger railway companies incorporated the viable operations of smaller ones. By the end of the 1860s, an extensive network of lines existed, and nearly all major population centres were connected to the rail network, many with more than one line and station, owned by different railway companies.[1] Atrocious safety standards and poor working conditions led to campaigns for nationalisation by trade unions and other civil society groups throughout the railways' first period of private ownership.

The outbreak of World War I in 1914 led to a need for a much more coordinated railway system than could be afforded by many small and overlapping private companies, and so the railway system was temporarily nationalised.[2] Nationalisation survived the war until the Railways Act 1921, when 120 railway companies were consolidated into four groups, thus creating the 'Big Four' railway companies, the Southern Railway, the Great Western Railway, the London Midland and Scottish Railway, and the London and North Eastern Railway. Many of the smaller railways were struggling financially. Amalgamation would bring the benefits of economies of scale and elimination of duplicate services.[3] During the inter-war years, the condition of the transport industry began to change. The railways faced increased competition from road hauliers, and economic recession meant a lowering of demand for lucrative freight traffic, seriously threatening the finances of the Big Four.[4]

Given their financial problems, the railways were in a sense saved by the outbreak of World War II, because they were renationalised for the war effort, playing a vital role in defending the nation from

Nazi invasion. But as a result of their intensive use and damage from bombing, and low levels of investment by private companies over many years, they ended the war in a terrible condition.[5]

Given the huge levels of investment needed, and the railways' difficulty in turning a profit, there could be no question of a return to private ownership after the war. The nationalisation of the railways in Britain in January 1948 was part of a package of measures to nationalise the 'commanding heights' of the economy.[6] British Railways (BR) was designed as a public service that would provide rail transport for freight and passengers free from the need to produce a profit, to underpin a significant expansion of the post-war economy.[7]

BR faced immediate operating losses, and would do so until its privatisation in the mid-1990s, save for two exceptional years in 1951 and 1953.[8] Operating losses were initially tolerated because of the benefits they accrued to the wider economy, but in 1956 the government stated that it wanted to 'turn the railways away from being just another nationalised industry into an organisation that functions on normal and sensible business lines'.[9] In other words, the railways would have to start to pay for themselves with the income they received from freight charges and passenger fares. This has essentially been the aspiration of every successive government since then, although some have been more patient than others to see the railways pay for themselves. Every conceivable approach has been taken.

The first attempt was through the 1955 Modernisation Plan. This created huge investment in infrastructure and rolling stock, including replacement of steam power by diesel and electric locomotives and upgrading of much of the mainline infrastructure. The idea was for short-term, high investment by the state to stimulate demand with higher-quality services, leading to greater fare revenue and profitability.[10] It was forecast that the plan would allow BR to completely eliminate the operating deficit by 1962.[11] However, its implementation failed to generate the level of revenue required to meet running costs, as passenger and freight income continued to decline. Its central flaw was the idea that, with investment, traffic could be won back from the roads, which under-estimated the popularity of the expanding road network and car ownership, although government policy – to instruct BR to hold down fares – did not help its financial position.[12]

By the 1960s, the government's impatience with BR's continued losses led to it imposing a new strategy on the company: instead of giving it money to invest in its services to generate increased income, BR would now have to make massive cuts to the network to reduce costs. In 1961 the government brought Richard Beeching into the management of BR. Beeching was an axeman, and the government gave him almost unlimited backing to take an unflinching approach to cost-cutting. He accordingly launched a review of BR's services. His plan proposed shutting down much of the national network, including 2,363 stations and 5,000 miles of track.[13] Cuts to lines and services continued well after Beeching's stewardship of BR, into the late 1960s and 1970s, and finally ended only in the 1980s, by which time the system had been reduced 'to a size which served proportionately fewer of Britain's towns and cities than comparable European systems'.[14] While it was probably necessary to trim the size of BR, particularly for the very lightly used lines, the Beeching and subsequent cuts were based on the fallacy that a profitable core network could be found with enough chopping of the branches. However, secondary services provide through traffic on the seemingly profitable routes; closing the former threatened the profitability of the latter. Indeed, BR's losses were greater during and immediately after the first Beeching cuts than in the preceding fourteen years.[15]

BR's losses were funded by intermittent bailouts by the Treasury. By the 1970s, elite thinking finally began to recognise what was common sense in other European countries – that the railways needed an annual subsidy to give them the stability necessary to provide the transport services required by industry and passengers. In 1974 the government introduced an annual state subsidy, while instructing BR that, henceforth, it should provide in the next year a service 'broadly comparable' to the level of service pertaining in the current year. Despite the government's recognition that BR required an annual subsidy, successive governments' intention was always to reduce subsidy levels as far as possible and aim towards profitability.[16]

In the 1980s Margaret Thatcher's New Right Conservative governments took to reducing BR's subsidy with particular zeal. For example, between 1983 and 1986, subsidy was cut by 25 per cent.[17] It was reduced through a series of reforms whereby BR was separated into quasi-businesses, creating the InterCity, Network South-East and Regional Railways brands. The reforms were aimed at distinguishing BR's 'commercially viable' services from those provided as a public service, in order to reduce the subsidy-draining effects of the latter.[18] Passenger numbers grew, through a combination of innovations in provision (such as the new High Speed Train), economic growth and a secular growth in demand for rail travel, prompted by new commuting patterns and road congestion.[19] Between 1983 and 1989 there was a growth in passenger income of 36 per cent,[20] and a 45 per cent decrease in subsidy.[21]

By the early 1990s, BR was arguably the most economically efficient of the Western European railway systems.[22] Subsidy began to climb again in the early 1990s. This was probably the result of a recession at the time. As one report argues, the dip in passenger revenue shows that, despite BR's heroic efficiency gains, railways remained 'a markedly cyclical business with semi fixed costs and volatile revenue'.[23] Despite this increase, subsidy remained low by historic standards.

But relatively low levels of subsidy for a basic level of service were not acceptable to John Major's Conservative government, elected in 1992. Major had a dream of privatising the railways in order to unleash the entrepreneurial flair of the private sector and reduce the government's financial and political responsibility for them. The privatisation of the railways was the last of the great privatisations undertaken by the Conservative governments of 1979–97. Major and other leading Conservative figures saw the selling-off of gas, water, electricity and telecommunication as a great success, creating high levels of customer focus while also bringing in sources of private finance to replace government investment. The government was proud of its ability to bring competitive pressures to what had been state-owned monopolies by breaking the industries up and creating new forms of regulation.[24]

As anyone who has used the railways in the recent past could guess, things would become much more complicated than the government could imagine. Although it was expected that new forms of competition would drive costs down, the government recognised that the railways would continue to require annual subsidy for at least the short to medium term. That would still mean an important role for government, despite its wish to get the railways off its hands. Moreover, competition was based on competing bids by private companies for government-sponsored contracts known as 'franchises' – something that had never been tested at scale on railways anywhere in the world. Most importantly, Major's government did not recognise, or admit, that the private sector would provide its own finance only if its returns were guaranteed by the state. That meant that any private money coming into the railways was not a free ticket, but had to eventually be paid back by the government – and usually at a much more expensive rate than if the government had borrowed the money directly.

Privatisation was just the latest attempt to reduce government responsibility for the railways and to get them to run as if they were commercial businesses, whose sole income comes from fares, rather than as a public service. Underlying the answers to my fellow passengers' questions is a simple argument. Privatisation was a particularly damaging example of decades of political elites trying to make the railways something they will never be again – commercially driven businesses free from government subsidy, rather than a public service whose state subsidy is justified by the enormous social and environmental benefits the railways provide. Not only has privatisation been a disaster for passengers; it has also created such a crisis of funding that the very future of the railways is now in serious doubt, at just the time when we need them most. What is more, the only people likely to do anything about it can be found on trains like ours: the passengers and the staff looking after them.

As my fellow passengers attest, there is something seriously wrong with our rail system. Commuters know this best, but so does anyone using the trains for leisure or more infrequent business travel. Trains are almost always more expensive to use than driving, and often more expensive than flying. They are often unreliable and late, they become overcrowded at times of high demand, and there is frequent industrial action which disrupts services. Our broken rail system blights the lives of Britain's railway passengers, but it is also a disaster for people who never use the railways, as the shambles forces people onto our already congested road network. We all deserve a much better railway system. That destination seems far out of reach. This book will show how we can get there.

Why don't the trains run on time?

Alisha's destination is Bolton, which requires a change at Manchester Piccadilly. Alisha is worried about whether she will make her connecting service and get home this evening. Her ten-year-old boy Adam is being looked after by her mother for the evening, but Adam can't stay over there – he has school in the morning, so he needs his uniform and other things from his house. Alisha is scrolling through various railway websites trying to find some clue as to when she might get to her mum's. With a sigh, she heavily places her phone on the table, apparently giving up.

'So, have you looked into why there are so many delays?' she asks me.

Alisha has been working as an account manager in central Manchester, part-time, for the past five years, commuting most days by train. There have been periods when she has been delayed almost every day, and countless times when she has been unable to board trains that are packed out thanks to delays and cancellations across the network.

'The thing is, it's been bad on the trains, but driving in is not really an option either', she tells me. In rush-hour traffic, driving can take up to an hour, as opposed to rail's advertised twenty-two-minute journey time, and parking is expensive in Manchester city centre.

The train should be the natural option for a traveller such as Alisha, but she's recently looked into buying a car, despite the costs involved.

'I've never needed one before, but I cannot go on like this with my job. My manager is really understanding – everyone knows that the trains are in a state. But the company are cracking down. The last thing I need is a disciplinary. I've worked hard to get where I am, and it's not easy to find work doing what I do.

'I've caught the train in other countries – Austria, Holland – and their trains always seem to be on time. If your book does anything, make sure it explains why the trains are always late. It needs sorting.'

Punctuality since privatisation

Railways in Britain have poor punctuality. No railway system is perfect (indeed, there is not a railway system in the world which does not require significant investment if countries are going to meet climate targets), and each is different. However, punctuality has been particularly poor on Britain's railways in comparison to other European countries. The UK is twenty-second of twenty-nine European countries in terms of rail punctuality.[1]

Moreover, the punctuality of services has worsened in recent years. Figure 1.1 shows that punctuality has declined significantly, with less than 87 per cent of trains running on time before the onset of Covid-19 in 2020. Note that 'on time' means trains arriving at their destination within five minutes of the scheduled time for short-distance services, and within ten minutes for long-distance services. These figures do not capture the severity of delays,

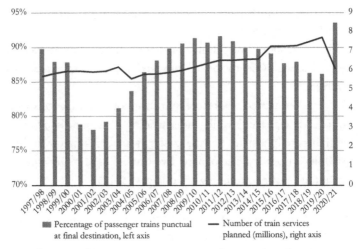

Figure 1.1 Passenger service provision and punctuality of services, 1997–2021.

mid-service late running or cancellations, so they represent a worse situation on the ground than is first apparent. However, they are useful for showing trends. By 2020, just before the Covid-19 outbreak, punctuality had been in steady decline for a decade, after some improvement in the late 2000s. It had fallen well below levels witnessed in 1997/98 – the year, shortly after privatisation, when punctuality began to be recorded this way. Delays are costing the British economy more than £1.5 billion a year.[2] Of course, these figures mask the very personal impact of delays and cancellations, as Alisha's experiences attest. And of course Alisha is not alone. One has to only think of the experiences of Lee Fenton, who lost his new job at Merton Council because Southern made him late for work three days in a row,[3] or Jonathan Lee-Smith, who moved from Blackpool to Devon to avoid having to use constantly delayed Northern services ever again.[4]

The capacity problem

The Covid-19 outbreak and subsequent lockdown greatly improved punctuality, despite increased levels of staff sick leave. Consideration of why that has been the case reveals a fundamental truth about delays: the more services that are provided, the less punctual they are. The significant reduction in services, responding to crashing demand as commuters began to work from home and leisure travel was all but obliterated, created the space on the network for much higher levels of punctuality than had been achieved since privatisation. It is impossible for any form of transport to provide a consistently on-time service – even the railways of Japan, celebrated for their punctuality, suffer from occasional delays.[5] But keeping enough spare capacity on the tracks helps enormously. Where services are too tightly packed together, a minor delay on one service starts a proverbial butterfly effect,[6] cascading delays across the network and sometimes reaching the other end of the country later in the day.[7]

The rising level of services over the past two decades is partly a result of an increase in demand for rail travel. As can be seen in Figure 1.2, the number of people travelling by train has increased substantially since the mid-1980s. Rising demand can be catered for in many ways. As we will see in Chapter 2, one of the main ways successive governments have managed demand is through increasing fares to deter travel. However, rail travel is often a 'distress purchase'. Like Alisha's commute to Manchester, most train journeys are non-discretionary: most people who choose the train do so because it is the most practical means of completing the journey, not primarily because of other concerns such as the environment.[8] Another 'solution' is to pack more passengers onto each service at peak times. Despite a significant increase in services over recent

13

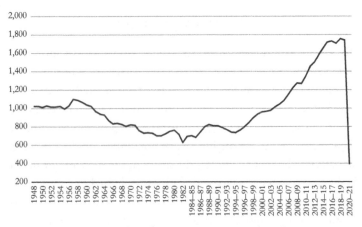

Figure 1.2 Number of passenger journeys made in Britain,
1948–2021 (millions).

years, overcrowding remained an endemic problem on the railways
until the outbreak of Covid-19, having increased by 84 per cent
between 1996 and 2019 in London and the south-east, for example, according to government figures.[9] There are limits to how
overcrowded services can be before passengers like Alisha get left
behind at stations – something that has been a common occurrence
in recent years.[10]

There are also limits to the extent to which extra services can be
provided without increasing the capacity of the infrastructure that
services operate on. This soon became apparent in the early years
of privatisation. The private train operating companies that took
over realised that there was an untapped demand for more frequent
services, following a decline in rail use that began to be reversed in
the mid-1980s.

Increasing demand was encouraged by government policy,
which reduced fares in the first years, partly in an attempt to popu-
larise privatisation. Train operating companies were incentivised to

provide more services by a steady decline in the government subsidy that they received, leaving a financial hole which only greater ticket sales could fill. Extra services were also incentivised by government policy, which deliberately held down the 'track access' fees that train operating companies needed to pay to use the railways' infrastructure.[11]

The increase in services meant that the infrastructure of tracks, bridges, tunnels and stations began to be used more intensively. This might not have been a problem if Railtrack – the post-privatisation owner of the infrastructure – had stepped up its maintenance regime to cope with the increased wear and tear additional services would cause. Railtrack's lack of maintenance was especially problematical because, in the last years of BR, the government had allowed the condition of the infrastructure to deteriorate, as part of an overall programme to cut public subsidy and allow the service to go further into decline, and so significant investment was needed in the infrastructure when the railways were privatised – not more cuts. As explained in the Introduction, successive governments' insistence that BR should turn a profit resulted in both periods of investment to boost usage and income, and periods of cuts to government support, in an attempt to stem losses, neither of which succeeded in making BR profitable. By the time of their privatisation in the mid-1990s, the railways had faced years of reorganisation, which had been extremely successful at increasing efficiency, but had also led to a decline in quality of track and trains.

In recognition of the fact that the infrastructure required substantial investment, the creation of Railtrack was seen as a way of breaking the direct link between the level of government subsidy given to the railways and the quality and quantity of infrastructure the railways could use. Railtrack was conceived as a shareholder-owned company, which could attract private finance that would be used to invest in infrastructure maintenance and expansion and earn returns on that investment from track access charges to train operating companies.[12]

Railtrack was to be regulated by a Rail Regulator, independent of both private rail companies and the government. Railways are regarded as 'natural monopolies'. A market economy is said to function most effectively if competition is unfettered. Competition relies on several companies each providing a similar product. Customers then choose who to buy from, and competition incentivises companies to undercut each other on price and improve the quality of products, both of which benefit customers. But for some industries, the sheer scale and cost of the infrastructure that they use make the duplication of that infrastructure practically impossible, and so competition is impossible to create. Competition is also difficult to organise in industries that rely on state funding. Competition assumes that there are 'customers' in the marketplace looking to buy goods and services. But who are the customers in state-subsidised industries? The service users, the government or both? Railways are a good example of an industry which is both a natural monopoly and utterly reliant on government funding. As such, they share some characteristics with roads. For example, it would be crazy to have competing motorways – the space for them does not exist, and government, the sole funder of motorways, would need to pay the huge extra costs of building and maintaining extra, parallel roads, unnecessarily increasing taxes. Competition just does not make any practical sense.

But John Major's rail-privatising Tory government, elected in 1992, had an obsession with competition. It believed that competition was a great way to improve publicly owned natural monopolies, which it was convinced were thoroughly inefficient, thanks to the managers of those industries lacking the discipline and incentives that profit motivation supposedly brings. Previous experiments with the privatisation of natural monopolies by governments – most importantly that of the electricity system – appeared to show that competition was beneficial to customers. It could be introduced by breaking the industry into pieces: the final delivery of services to consumers could consist of competing companies in a 'market', even if the core infrastructure enabling that provision had to remain as a monopoly. This was exactly the thinking behind the separation of passenger services and infrastructure provision. Infrastructure provision formed the only part of the privatised railway system to remain a true monopoly, while various forms of competition could be created in the other parts of the system, including competition between private train operating companies to win government-sponsored 'franchise' contracts for the right to run passenger rail services on Railtrack's infrastructure.

The Rail Regulator was tasked with preventing two major types of market abuse open to monopolies: overcharging and underproviding. Accordingly, it set 'track access charges' and minimum standards for infrastructure maintenance. The regulator would be able to issue fines if Railtrack's performance fell below the level expected.[13]

According to the theory behind rail privatisation, regulation, together with the private investment that privatisation promised, should have ensured that Railtrack provided a good-quality infrastructure, and with less public subsidy than had been required by BR.[14] However, Railtrack's management was more interested in paying dividends to shareholders than it was in paying for the maintenance and improvement of infrastructure. Between the floatation of Railtrack on the stock market in 1996, and 2000, Railtrack paid £1.1 billion to its shareholders.[15]

In stark contrast with Railtrack's impressive ability to reward shareholders was its neglect of maintaining the infrastructure. Such neglect was evident early on in Railtrack's existence. The Rail Regulator complained in 1996 that Railtrack had underspent on maintenance by £700 million. As a result, it issued an 'enforcement notice' requiring an improvement in the company's performance.[16] The regulator subsequently rebuked Railtrack for making 'very few commitments' to improve and expand the infrastructure.[17] The company was clearly deliberately reducing its maintenance spending to save money. A damning report compiled in 1999 for the regulator found that there had been a long-term decline in Railtrack's 'assets', meaning track and other infrastructure.[18] An investigation by the National Audit Office highlighted one of the consequences of underspending on track maintenance: the number of broken rails had increased by 25 per cent during the 1997/98 financial year. The regulator had been aware of the problem of the deterioration of track quality, and in 1998 urged Railtrack to improve maintenance.[19]

Railtrack's neglect of the infrastructure was brutally exposed in a train crash on 17 October 2000, at Hatfield in Hertfordshire on the East Coast Main Line. The crash was highly significant, not just in terms of what it revealed about the failings of the privatisation of infrastructure, but also because it prompted significant changes to the way infrastructure was managed, which have important consequences to this day.

An express London-to-Leeds train, travelling at around 115 miles per hour, derailed from the track. The derailment caused the loss of four lives and injuries to over seventy others.[20] It was discovered that the crash had resulted from a cracked rail. Because Railtrack lacked an 'asset register', it was unaware of the true condition of the track at the crash site. Under BR, track maintenance workers had kept to particular sections of route, meaning that they carried knowledge of track conditions around in their heads. This was not the case, however, after privatisation. Railtrack's use of subcontracting for track maintenance destroyed that local knowledge, making its failure to create and maintain an asset register a fatal one.[21]

By the time of the Hatfield crash, the Conservatives had been replaced in government by New Labour under the leadership of Tony Blair. The Labour Party had been highly critical of rail privatisation while in opposition, and promised significant improvements to the railways in its 1997 general election manifesto.[22] There were two planks to its policy: increased public and private investment, and stronger and more effective regulation. Implicit in its plan was a notion that private rail companies, not least Railtrack, were taking the public and taxpayer for a ride. But rather than push for the most obvious solution – renationalisation – New Labour felt that the best bet was to bear down on the worst excesses of private greed and irresponsibility though tougher regulation. So the incoming New Labour government appointed Tom Winsor, a combative lawyer specialising in monopoly regulation. Immediately taking up this task with gusto, Winsor issued Railtrack with warnings and fines for lack of attention to track maintenance.

Yet, while New Labour had identified some of privatisation's shortcomings, its solutions fell short of fixing them and could not prevent the disaster of Hatfield. How come? Any private company needs access to finance, which it can use to invest and turn a profit. Financial investors are then able to earn a return on their investments. Money for investment can be obtained either by issuing shares or by borrowing from banks and other financial institutions. Failure to reward investment means risking not being able to access finance in the future, so loan repayments and shareholder dividends must be maintained. Thus any regulator, including Winsor, was obliged to consider the financial position of Railtrack when setting its income.[23] This made the issuance of fines – the Rail Regulator's ultimate action of recourse – unrealistic beyond a certain token level, because too heavy a fine would hurt Railtrack's shareholders, making the business financially unviable. So Railtrack was essentially allowed to get away with inadequate maintenance and failure to keep an up-to-date asset register, both of which were key causes of the Hatfield crash.

But the underlying problem continued to be government's lack of willingness to fund an unprofitable but economically indispensable industry. New Labour had genuinely high ambitions for public transport at the beginning of its period of political dominance in the late 1990s. John Prescott, New Labour's first transport secretary, had grand plans for an 'integrated transport system', which he published in July 1998.[24] Prescott recognised that decades of transport policy, centred on building more and more roads to cater for an ever-greater demand by motorists, had to end. Road building had not solved congestion and transport-related environmental problems. Indeed, it had only served to induce demand, creating a vicious cycle of more roads, more cars and more congestion. The only solution was to create a public transport system that was able to compete with the convenience of driving by being comprehensive, seamless and accessible.[25]

This was compelling stuff. The problem: how to pay for it? Because as enthusiastic and forward-thinking as Prescott's proposals were, to have any chance of seeing the light of day they would need to get past the door of the Iron Chancellor himself, chancellor of the exchequer Gordon Brown. New Labour had set its stall on 'economic proficiency'. Brown had pledged to keep within the previous Conservative government's austere spending plans, to not increase tax on the highest earners and to self-impose strict financial rules, which would prevent the government borrowing money to fund spending.[26] Brown's adherence to his self-imposed rules put up insurmountable roadblocks to Prescott's transport ambitions.

The same policy dilemma was faced in the immediate aftermath of the Hatfield crash, once New Labour had been in power for three years, but this time it was worse. Without an asset register to hand to identify where on the network there were similar cracks in the rails, severe speed restrictions had to be imposed nationwide to allow survey teams to check every centimetre of rail. This caused immense disruption for months during the remainder of 2000 and into 2001. The speed restrictions vastly reduced the railways' income, as services became almost completely unreliable right across the country. However, the railways' loss of income from fares was but a drop in the ocean compared with the enormous costs of rebuilding an infrastructure which was on its last legs before privatisation and had been finally broken by increased use and lack of routine maintenance by Railtrack.

The New Labour government seemed to face a stark choice: to cut its losses and renationalise the infrastructure, or to let the railways go to the wall. Although renationalisation was the simplest thing to do, it would destroy Brown's plans to keep within his financial rules. The 'solution' was classic New Labour – a 'third way' was found which took advantage of innovation and appetite for lending in international financial markets, by using private finance to square the circle of low taxes and improved public services.[27] After months of negotiations between private rail companies, international investment funds and banks, and Brown's Treasury, the government came up with 'Network Rail', which took over the ownership and management of infrastructure in 2002.

Legally speaking, Network Rail was a private company. But, unlike most private companies, it had neither owners nor shareholders.[28] The strangeness of this set-up is explained by the benefits it brought the government. In 2003 Tom Winsor, the Rail Regulator, told the government in his review of Network Rail's income requirements that £24.9 billion was required to restore the infrastructure to a good condition and cater for the overall rise in demand for rail services expected in the period from 2004/05 to 2008/09.[29] This sum was far higher than the government was expecting or could afford within Brown's financial rules – around £7.4 billion higher, according to Winsor – and there was great pressure on the regulator from government ministers to reduce Network Rail's income.[30] Winsor made clear to them what the effect would be of keeping rail spending within the government's pre-existing budget, telling the government that the size of the rail network would need to be dramatically reduced, meaning no services

> ... in Wales, apart from Cardiff, nothing in Scotland, apart from Edinburgh and Glasgow, and a lot [of other cuts to the network] besides. You're going to have to reduce the amount of passenger and freight traffic on the remaining network by a further 25 per cent; you're going to have to cut the entire enhancement budget; you're going to have to cut renewals; your maintenance budget is going to rocket – because things are going to be wearing out, and you won't be renewing them, and you certainly won't be enhancing them; performance is going to fall like a stone; and you're going to have to have a 6 per cent year-on-year real terms increase on passenger fares.[31]

But Network Rail's private-sector status meant that it would be able to borrow from international private financial investors to pay for much of this work, so preventing the government itself from having to do so directly. Network Rail also received a guarantee from government to lenders that the government would step in to pay off Network Rail's debts in the event that Network Rail were to default on loan repayments. This meant that Network Rail could borrow at lower interest rates, and nearly (but not quite) at the rates at which the government itself could borrow. It was an accounting trick which allowed the government to borrow money to help pay for the massive costs of fixing the infrastructure, without Brown's financial rules being breached.[32]

And it worked, in a way. After Network Rail's takeover from Railtrack, annual spending on the infrastructure rose from £6 billion a year to £9 billion twelve years later, in today's prices. After a relative dearth of infrastructure spending by Railtrack in the years leading up to the Hatfield crash, under Network Rail spending was finally matching the increased demand, and use, of railways by passengers (see Figure 1.3).[33] The effect on punctuality was considerable, as can be seen in Figure 1.1. It raised 'on time' arrivals from 78 per cent in 2001, in the immediate post-Hatfield meltdown period,

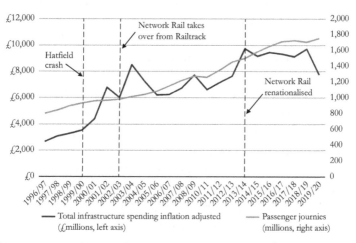

Figure 1.3 Real-terms infrastructure spending (2021 prices) and passenger journeys over time, 1996–2020.

to as much as 92 per cent ten years later. This matched once again the level of punctuality the railways were achieving when they were privatised, despite a 27 per cent increase in services provided and a 73 per cent increase in passenger journeys made.[34] Although this level of punctuality was not near the achievements of many other European railways, it was a significant improvement, and a return to a more usable and reliable railway.

But New Labour's new tracks were built on sand. With Network Rail fully established from October 2002, it undertook huge amounts of borrowing to pay for the restoration and, in some cases, improvement of the infrastructure to meet increasing demand for rail travel.

For a normal company, increased borrowing can be justified if income is projected to increase as a result of the investment. But Network Rail's income was reliant on government subsidy. So Network Rail's debt *had to* keep increasing, or else government spending would have to increase, and that would have worked against New Labour's debt-financed 'solution' to fixing the railways and restoring punctuality after Hatfield. For a normal company, ever-increasing debt would increase the company's cost of borrowing, as creditors would deem it riskier to lend to. But Network Rail had the government guarantee, allowing it to continually return to debt markets for more and more money – a situation some commentators referred to as the railways' 'credit card'.[35] As a result, the company's interest obligations increased massively as it took on ever more debt, not just to pay for day-to-day costs, but to cover the interest payments on previous loans. From 2011 the company was spending more on interest payments to service its debts than it was spending on maintaining the infrastructure.[36]

Something had to give. At some point, the ridiculousness of what was in reality a government-owned and government-controlled company taking on exponentially higher levels of debt, mostly in the service of keeping the railways running, had to end. That denouement came in September 2014, when a change in European Union (EU) accounting rules forced the then Conservative-led coalition government of David Cameron to legally renationalise Network Rail.

Renationalisation was a disaster for Cameron's government. It forced an astronomical £34 billion onto the public balance sheet,[37] at a time when severe cuts to public expenditure were the order of the day, with the country still reeling from the global financial crisis and with 'austerity' – involving vast cuts to spending on public services and welfare – preferred to increasing taxes on the wealthy.

Network Rail's renationalisation was to have big implications for the capacity of the infrastructure to support punctual services. It could no longer borrow from the private sector, and so the government had to step in to make up the shortfall with its own loans.[38] However, the term 'loan' in this context is government spin. Given that Network Rail was renationalised, the loans were simply cash payments from one arm of government to another. In reality, they represented more than a doubling of government subsidy, from around £6 billion a year to around £13 billion (see Figure 1.4).[39] In real terms, public subsidy was now around four times higher than it had been in the latter days of BR.

In 2015, with the private finance taps turned off and desperately seeking ways to lower the huge public subsidy bill, the then Conservative majority government of David Cameron launched a report into the funding of Network Rail, led by industry insider Nicola Shaw. Shaw made some useful observations, not least on the need for greater regional planning in order to take the railways away from the overbearing influence of civil servants in Whitehall.

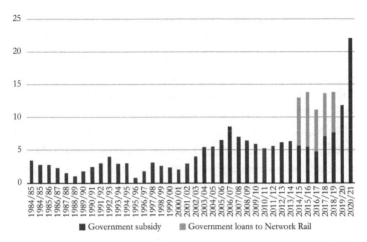

Figure 1.4 Government subsidy to the railways, 1984–2021
(constant 2020/21 prices).

According to Patrick Butcher, the chief financial officer of Network Rail from 2009 to 2015, the renationalisation of Network Rail meant that its spending was now much more controlled by central government, and:

> … instead of Network Rail being able to make decisions and get on with it, decisions needed to go up through the DfT [Department for Transport], and they'd go up three layers of the DfT, and then sometimes [the] Treasury or even the Cabinet Office, taking months to get decisions made which we could have made more quickly.[40]

But Shaw failed at her principal goals – to get the government out of its railway financial bind, and get the railways out of their government bind. Although she suggested that there might be new opportunities to use private finance to maintain and improve the infrastructure, no concrete ideas were forthcoming.

To be fair, she was given an impossible task: since privatisation, successive governments had attempted all kinds of institutional and accounting chicanery to reduce public subsidy while meeting increased demand for rail travel. But they had run out of tricks. By dismissing the railways' need for substantial public subsidy and using private finance to plug the gap, governments stored up huge debts that were met by ever more private borrowing. Finally, by 2015, this crazy dynamic had been brought to an end. But there was no public policy to replace the old one.

The result was a review of the now nationalised Network Rail's spending plans in 2015, led by chairman Sir Peter Hendy. Hendy identified a number of projects at advanced stages of planning, designed to increase capacity through such measures as electrification, which would need to be curtailed. Although many of these schemes were running over budget, as the report makes clear, the principal motivation for the report was to identify the financial consequences for the government of Network Rail's renationalisation. Whereas previously Network Rail's access to private finance was seemingly unlimited, now that its borrowing was to be counted as government borrowing, it had to operate within very strict Treasury-determined public borrowing limits.

In other words, the Hendy review made clear that many of the projects designed to deliver real improvements in capacity, which were desperately needed in order to make the railways more reliable and punctual, needed to be kicked into the long grass in a desperate attempt to control the railways' now enormous public subsidy costs. As can be seen in Figure 1.3, infrastructure spending started on a downward trend. The result was the cancellation or curtailment of infrastructure projects which, as demand for travel continued to rise, would have helped to alleviate the railways' capacity crisis and bring down delays overall.[41]

The train crew problem

Although the infrastructure of the railways is very important, it is people who keep the system running and provide a vital point of human contact and support for the millions of passengers who use Britain's railways every year. Alisha tells me that she frequently finds a train waiting at the platform which is ready to go but cannot because of 'a shortage of train crew'. Although official statistics show that train-crew-related problems account for only around 9 per cent of total delays,[42] they become particularly problematic as a knock-on effect of disruption: a late Service A means that there is no crew to operate Service B, and so on.[43]

Train operating companies are quick to blame staff shortages on staff sickness and other forms of 'absenteeism'.[44] But lack of train crew has persistently been the second highest contributor to delays to services caused by train operating companies in recent years.[45] This suggests that it is an ongoing problem, with long-standing underlying causes – not, as the train companies subtly imply, that delays are the result of rail workers becoming lazy or irresponsible.

To understand why trains keep being left at platforms by staff absence, you need to know something about their employers – the train operating companies. Train operating companies are essentially outsourced providers for government contracts – the franchises. As we have seen, train operating companies do not own infrastructure: this is accessed by paying the infrastructure provider (first Railtrack, later Network Rail). But they also do not own the rolling stock they use: this is leased from rolling stock companies, which are owned by a plethora of international private financial institutions.

Chapter 2 will deal with the rolling stock companies in more detail. The important thing to note here is that their existence means that train operating companies own very little capital as such – their main role in the railway system is to manage services and to provide the staff for them. But let us recall that the main motivation behind privatisation was to save money. What was the train operating companies' role in achieving that aim supposed to be? Since the costs of using the infrastructure and rolling stock are not determined by the train operating companies, the only place where they can hope to make savings is in their use of staff. It is largely through reducing spending on staff, which makes up only 29 per cent of train operating companies' total operating expenditure,[46] that bidders for franchises hope to find a cutting edge over their rivals. Train operating companies are therefore incentivised to reduce the number of staff on their salary books.

The resulting cuts mean that there are fewer staff to cover for staff sickness. This is particularly problematic in the case of train drivers. Train operating companies are reluctant to train up new drivers, because of the high costs and long lead time involved in doing so. This is not so much of a problem for state-owned railway systems, where the high cost of training drivers can be recovered over the many years the driver works on the railways. It is more challenging for private train operating companies, whose financial interests are limited to the length of franchise contracts, which are typically much shorter than the working life of a driver. So instead of focussing on training new drivers, train operating companies tend to try to 'poach' drivers from each other. The result is a long-term undersupply of drivers in the industry as a whole,[47] and therefore less cover in times of disruption.

This is not to say that new drivers are never recruited by train operating companies. If that were the case, there would be very few drivers on the national network, and all of them close to retirement. But thanks to the financial incentives they face, recruitment is the last option train operating companies will usually go for.

The other part of the train crew are the guards. Guards are cheaper than drivers, and take less time to train. In addition, the role of the guards has to a great extent been made secure by trade union organisation, which has prevented train operating companies from cutting guard numbers as much as they, and the government, would like (see Chapter 3). Nevertheless, trains cannot run with guards alone, and the persistent driver shortage is a symptom of the corner-cutting and short-termism that has ruled the railways for decades.

The fragmentation problem

In some cases, a planned expansion of services creates a need for a substantial number of extra staff, requiring a big recruitment drive. One such plan was a great expansion of services in the north of England from 2016. It was the disastrous implementation of the plan, which produced a cascade of problems for the rail operations, that nearly cost Alisha her job in 2018.

In 2015 Arriva, a subsidiary of Deutsche Bahn, Germany's state-owned rail company, won the bid to operate the next Northern franchise. The media hailed a '£1.2bn upgrade boost' to services across the north of England which the award promised.[48] Awarding the franchise was a key part of the Great North Rail Project, which planned to increase capacity by introducing 'brand new trains, including more than 500 new carriages' which would create 'room for 40,000 extra passengers and more than 2,800 extra services a week'.[49] Arriva promised to invest £400 million in new trains that would add 40 per cent extra capacity to services which were straining from overcrowding. The transport secretary Patrick McLoughlin stated that 'As a one-nation government we are committed to closing the economic gap between north and south.

This deal ... will bring the northern powerhouse to life.'[50] The Great North Rail Project promised to lead to improvements in the reliability of services,[51] and the award of the Northern franchise to Arriva promised to significantly contribute to this.[52]

But thanks to the fragmentation of the railways, far from delivering promised improvements to services, the introduction of the new timetable on 20 May 2018, which was supposed to bring immediate benefits for millions of passengers, rapidly increased delays and cancellations. Alisha was not alone. During this period up to 11 per cent of scheduled services were cancelled across the Northern network each weekday.[53] The punctuality of Northern had been far from ideal before, but the timetable change on 20 May doubled delays to services. Punctuality did stabilise somewhat by 4 June, but only by removing 165 services through an emergency timetable.[54] But cuts to services, to ensure that some basic level of punctuality could be provided, continued for months and years to come. Right through to when the Covid-19 pandemic hit Britain in early 2020, Northern services were routinely cancelled at weekends, seemingly with the support of the Department for Transport.[55]

Railways are unlike roads in that their services have to be carefully planned to maximise capacity without over-burdening the network. So timetable planning is crucial to ensure that trains are as punctual as they can be. The plan was that after a couple of years of preparation, a huge number of new services would be introduced onto the Northern network at the same time, all starting on 20 May 2018. Introducing new services requires not just a new timetable, but new rolling stock, new infrastructure and new staff. This is a very complex process to manage, with an array of independent variables. The timetable changes themselves were highly ambitious, affecting around four times the number of services usually re-cast in one go. Including changes to south of London services (on the Govia Thameslink Railway franchise), they accounted for 46 per cent of all services nationally.

Unpicking the reasons behind the 2018 timetable chaos has been the complex task of both a parliamentary inquiry and investigations by the Rail Regulator. However, a brief run-down of events shows that the key problem was the fragmentation of the rail industry – a problem which has dogged many attempts to meet increased demand without making the punctuality of services worse.

Northern's plans for vastly increased services were dependent on Network Rail's big projects to increase capacity in the north-west, not least the electrification projects that had survived Hendy's cuts to infrastructure enhancement projects after Network Rail's rena-tionalisation. Electrification promised to finally bring lines built in the nineteenth century up to modern standards. As well as being better for the environment, electrification increases the acceleration of trains, meaning greater capacity and fewer delays. However, in the new year of 2018, Network Rail informed Northern that a sub-stantial amount of the work would not be completed by the time-table change date of 20 May, so a new timetable would be required. But this gave Northern just sixteen weeks, rather than the usual forty, to come up with one. Network Rail refused a request from Northern to delay the timetable change to allow for infrastructure work to be completed. As a subsequent parliamentary inquiry sug-gests, it is likely that Northern's request was ultimately refused by senior ministers,[56] perhaps to avoid the political embarrassment of delayed improvements to services.

In anticipation of the new timetable, Northern had entered into contracts with rolling stock leasing companies to supply electrically powered vehicles. These were due to run on the newly electrified lines, while the existing diesel trains on those lines could be rede-ployed to bolster services in other parts of the network. Delays to electrification meant that Northern effectively had, in the words of one Department for Transport official, 'a missing train fleet'.[57] The result was cancellations and shorter trains across the network. To make matters worse, the delay to electrification meant that, in order to continue driving trains on the Northern routes, around 450 drivers had to be taken off driving duties and retrained, causing a shortfall just as the new timetable came into operation.[58]

A subsequent report into the calamity by the Rail Regulator found that, although there were many factors at play, the principal reason for the disruption was a lack of accountability and responsibility in the industry for addressing 'systemic risks'. In a complex industry, things will not always go to plan. So it is vitally important that the risk of service meltdown is identified early, and alternative plans made, to give passengers plenty of notice of any changes to services. But 'nobody took charge', partly because it was not clear who should do so.[59]

A subsequent cross-party parliamentary inquiry rightly went further, making clear that it is ultimately the transport secretary's responsibility to ensure that good-quality rail services are provided. However, such responsibility is difficult to take in a 'fragmented, over-complicated system, with competing contractual interests'.[60] To be clear, these contractual interests were Northern's franchise contract with the Department for Transport, Northern's contract for trains with private leasing companies, Northern's contracts with its staff (including drivers) and Network Rail's contracts with private construction firms working on infrastructure upgrades. The May 2018 Northern Rail debacle showed that the fragmentation of the railways makes it very difficult to coordinate big investments to improve services, including their punctuality, and makes them much more likely to cause severe disruption to passengers in the short to medium term.

Conclusion

Successive governments have attempted to save money on the railways by chopping them into pieces, attempting to generate competition and attracting private finance. This has led to several outcomes, all of which make Alisha's regular train more likely to be late. First, the system does not have the infrastructure to cope with the level of passengers' demand for services, and so more services are squeezed onto the network than it can cope with. This is a direct result of years of successive governments using private finance to plug holes in the rail budget. The effect has been much higher public subsidy, and therefore less chance that government will fund expansion and improvements to the infrastructure, especially now that the private money taps have been turned off. Second, any disruption on the network is compounded by deliberate understaffing by train operating companies, which is an inevitable result of a franchising model where competition between private operators in bidding for franchise contracts rests on each bidder's confidence in being able to run services with the smallest possible number of staff. Finally, creating competition and private finance requires splitting the industry into pieces. Straightforward competition between rail companies is not possible, because rail infrastructure cannot be duplicated, and private financial investors wish to invest in discrete, 'profitable' parts of the industry, leaving the rest to be directly subsidised by the taxpayer. The ensuing fragmentation of operations creates incoherence and duplication across an industry that has struggled to meet growing demand for rail travel.

For those keen on privatisation, many of these problems could be ironed out with the installation of a 'guiding mind' or 'fat controller' – some kind of individual or organisation which could unite these disparate parts and take responsibility for both the day-to-day performance of services and longer-term plans to improve capacity and reliability. For those who have this view, there is no reason why different parts of the rail system cannot be owned, or run by, private companies.[61]

But this leaves some unanswered questions: in a system absolutely reliant on public subsidy, what is the point of private-sector involvement when private companies must reward their shareholders, which increases the overall industry costs that must be passed on to passengers and taxpayers? If it is not to save money, then there must be something else that private involvement brings. It is unlikely to be a different set of workers, since there is only a limited pool of trained and competent workers who are available for most railway tasks – they are not easily or cheaply replaced.[62] What we are left with is a certain *je ne sais quoi* – an entrepreneurial spirit, free from the fetters of civil service interference. Yet in a system constrained both by limits in public subsidy and by the inevitable government interference which comes with it, there is surely little room for out-of-the-box thinking. What is more, there are few successful examples of private-sector involvement in complex, statefunded industries. Outsourcing in the National Health Service, social care and education has been a disaster. What basis is there to assume that it will not continue to be so on the railways?[63]

The increased costs created by privatisation – which have resulted from successive governments' addiction to private finance for reducing public subsidy in the short term – have led to an unreliable and overcrowded railway. As we will see in the next chapter, they have also led to horrendous fare rises and the pricing of former and prospective rail passengers off the railways altogether.

Why are fares so high?

Our train starts moving again, making a spirited departure from Milton Keynes, much to everyone's relief. However, just before Lichfield Trent Valley, we grind to a halt again. The train manager comes on the public address system again, to uselessly inform us that we will be further delayed, but for a period unknown.

'Considering how much you pay, it's a joke', Sam declares. 'Ninety-four pounds. Return to Stockport.' Sam has to pass these costs on to his clients, who are dependent on the highly specialised form of physiotherapy he offers.

'Yeah, my mum got a flight from London to Glasgow the other day', Ruth responds. 'I said, "Why're you doing that – by the time you've got to the airport and checked in, you'd be most the way there on the train." Turns out the train costs twice the price of the plane. That's insane.'

'So that's another thing', says Sam. 'Why do tickets cost so much?'

Rip-off railways

Britain's rail fares are too expensive, and that expense excludes many people who would otherwise be willing to leave that car at home, and denies travel altogether to people who lack alternative means of transport, especially the poorest in our society.

Fewer than half of railway passengers are satisfied with the price of their ticket.[1] Little wonder, given that Britain has some of the highest fares for train travel in Europe. Some of the passengers on our train are on their way back from a day trip to London. Those who arrived in London before 11:30 in the morning will have paid £369.40 for an anytime return from Manchester in standard class. By contrast, you will not pay more than £115 for a peak return from Hanover to Berlin, a journey of similar distance (with discounts possible for booking in advance).[2] Indeed, one research report found that, of the eight major European countries studied, Britain has the highest peak fares, the highest anytime fares, the highest off-peak fares (except for short distances, where it came second to Germany), and the most expensive season tickets.[3]

The train operating companies' trade body, the Rail Delivery Group, excuses this situation, claiming that 'while Britain [has] relatively high fares for some types of journeys compared to other countries in Europe, it also [has] some of the lowest ticket prices for long distance journeys with operators now selling more and more cheap tickets'.[4] Indeed, it is a common tactic of apologists for Britain's exorbitantly priced railways to claim that there are great bargains to be had if passengers take the time to 'shop around' and make the right choices according to their travel needs and budget.[5] For example, in 2015 the then rail minister, Claire Perry, argued that while the latest above-inflation rise in rail fares were needed for investment, 'you can get travel from Manchester to London for £15'. Subsequent research by Transport Focus found no journeys for that price for the next three months – the extent of the booking window on that route.[6]

There is a grain of truth in the idea that very low fares are available through advance purchasing. Advance tickets are a way of filling trains at times of lower demand, similar to how airlines tickets are sold. This has indeed opened up some good-value fares to some passengers, although advance tickets were introduced by BR and are not an innovation of private rail companies, as privatisation's supporters often suggest.[7] Furthermore, only 5 per cent of journeys are made using advance tickets,[8] meaning that the vast majority of travellers are unable to take advantage of these discounted fares – hardly a surprise when they are for filling spare seats on a highly congested network.

The 'great bargains' myth is used to justify ever-increasing fare rises, by giving the false impression that cheap fares can be easily found. In reality, most passengers have little choice in when they need to travel, and the rail industry exploits that to maximise revenue.

The story of the never-ending fare rise

Under public ownership, fares were set by BR. For most of BR's existence, fares remained roughly level, when inflation is taken into account. In the 1980s BR's fares policy began to focus more on saving public subsidy. To do this, BR introduced a range of off-peak tickets to fill less busy services; peak fares captured extra revenue from business travellers, and season tickets could save money for regular commuters.[9] Higher peak fares dampened demand at busy times, which saved the government from having to make significant investments to expand infrastructure.

More attractive fares were supposed to be one of the main benefits of privatisation. Proponents claimed that competition between companies to run passenger services would increase the efficiency of operations, and that the resulting reduction in costs would allow reduced fares alongside lower state subsidy, higher levels of investment and, of course, a margin for profit.[10]

Privatisation's promoters envisaged that the cost of travel would be entirely determined by supply and demand.[11] However, shortly before privatisation, it became clear that a fare free-for-all was out of the question. Instead, the government chose to regulate fares by setting maximum prices that train operating companies could charge for particular types of ticket. These included commuter fares and longer-distance intercity 'leisure' fares, which account for around half of fare income taken by train operating companies.[12] The Major government was keen to rush privatisation through before the 1997 general election, and so fare regulation was offered as a sop to sceptical MPs, who were worried that privatisation would mean passengers with no alternative means of transport being priced off the railways.[13] So the government committed itself to increasing rail fares only in line with inflation. Better still, it determined that in the first years of the privatised system's operation, between 1998 and 2003, regulated fares would increase 1 per cent *below* inflation – a real-terms cut.[14]

Since 2003, and in the teeth of the railways' financial crisis following the Hatfield crash, government policy has deliberately shifted the financial burden of running the railways from itself to passengers, using fare regulation – which was supposed to protect passengers – to achieve that goal. The Strategic Rail Authority – the Blair government's public body responsible for managing the railways – argued that 'increasing industry costs have [since privatisation] been borne almost entirely by the taxpayer', and so, because 'realistically, there are only two sources of funds for the railway – fares ... and subsidy', it was therefore time to 'redress the balance between taxpayer and passenger'.[15] Of course, this left the other interested financial parties – shareholders and bondholders – conveniently outside the discussion, despite their involvement having been largely responsible for increasing the railways' income requirements. The Blair government's policy change shifted the financial burden on passengers for funding the railways from around one third of railway income to around two thirds, with the proportion of government contributions running in the opposite direction.[16] Privatisation vastly increased costs and sent the system into meltdown: now passengers would have to pick up the tab.

To make things even worse, the government's chosen inflation benchmark for fare regulation – the retail price index (RPI) – over-estimates real inflation. Inflation is a measure of what you can buy with a given amount of money, and RPI over-estimates increases in costs faced by households for a number of commonly purchased goods and services. Such is the unsuitability of RPI that it was abandoned as an official measure of inflation in 2013, and the more accurate Consumer Prices Index (now referred to as CPIH because it now includes housing costs) preferred.[17]

When inflation is considered appropriately, the result, as can be seen in Figure 2.1, is that train travel has become more expensive every year since the beginning of privatisation in 1996. Standard class fares have increased by 135 per cent between 1996 and 2021. Adjusted for the government-preferred RPI inflation measure, that is a 16 per cent increase, but according to the CPIH measure, it's a whopping 40 per cent.

Around 45 per cent of all fares are regulated, and the rest are set by the train operating companies themselves. Despite successive governments using fare regulation to push the costs of rail transport onto passengers, regulation remains a brake on otherwise even more excessive increases. As Figure 2.2 shows, unregulated fares

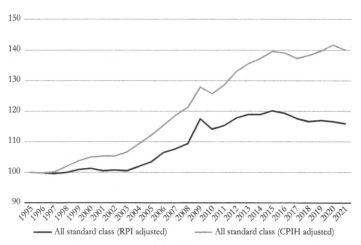

Figure 2.1 Standard class rail fare price changes, 1995–2021, RPI and CPIH adjusted.

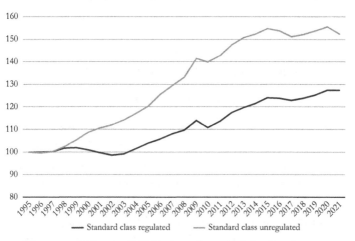

Figure 2.2 Real-terms (CPIH adjusted) standard class fare changes, 1995–2021.

have increased by 52 per cent in real terms since 1995, as opposed to the 27 per cent increase in regulated fares. For over half of fares available, there has been nothing to stop rail companies bumping up prices as much as they think they can get away with, taking advantage of increased demand and lack of investment in improving capacity.

Despite the rail industry's spin, fares have increased massively over the past twenty-five years, and this has been detrimental for the vast majority of passengers. Bargain advance fares act as an ideological smokescreen which allows rail companies and the government political cover for rinsing the travelling public.

One consequence of the bargain fare fallacy that has been used to justify privatisation is the sheer complexity of fares that it has created. As will be seen in the next section, this has been cynically leveraged by train operating companies to criminalise rail passengers ensnared by a baffling proliferation of rules and restrictions.

The Kafkaesque world of buying a train ticket

The secret cheaper tickets

Passengers are faced with a bewildering range of ticket choices, accompanied by poor information on each ticket's validity. A survey commissioned by the Rail Regulator found that 52 per cent of passengers agreed that 'it is a bit of a lottery as to whether you find the best price for a rail journey or not'. Indeed, 41 per cent have bought tickets in the past only to find later that cheaper options were available, and 15 per cent have boarded a train with an invalid ticket, meaning that a new one had to be purchased.[18] Overall, passengers find that the fares structure is 'complicated, confusing and illogical'.[19] According to one study, up to 35 per cent of people who do not travel by train have been put off by the complexity of fares.[20]

Part of the reason fares are so complicated is the array of differ-ent standard ticket types on offer,[21] from various types of walk-on single fare (anytime, off-peak), return (anytime, anytime day, off-peak, off-peak day), season tickets, rovers, special offer tickets and so on. Some of this complexity was present when the railways were privatised, but it was made much worse by allowing private train operating companies to offer walk-on and advance tickets solely for use on their own services.

Passengers buy tickets from an array of websites and apps, at station ticket offices and on trains. In theory, all ticket vendors are supposed to offer advice on the most suitable ticket for a pas-senger's journey, including details of the cheapest fares available.[22] However, in practice, many passengers are paying more for their journeys than they need to.

For example, a passenger wishing to make a return journey from Plymouth to Aberdeen, leaving on Friday morning and return-ing on Sunday morning, would be likely to find the 09:27 Cross Country service from Plymouth a useful one, as it is the only direct train of the day. If the small number of advance seats are already sold, Cross Country will quote the walk-on fare. This comes out at a scarcely believable £462.60. The passenger is offered that fare because the departure time of 09:27 is three minutes before off-peak tickets can be used on a weekday. However, the same passenger can make the same journey by buying an off-peak return from Totnes to Aberdeen for £272.10, plus a single from Plymouth to Totnes and a single from Totnes to Plymouth at £7.10 each, for a combined price of £286.30. That's because, by the time the passenger's train reaches Totnes, it's past 09:30, and off-peak fares are allowed to Aberdeen. Passengers are allowed to hold a combination of tickets for their journeys, the only proviso being that their train must stop at the station where the tickets meet up, and there is no need to get off the train and back on it.

So passengers can save £176.30 on this journey by having an awareness of ticket rules, but 'split tickets' such as these are not marketed by the train operating companies' websites. Split tickets are often called 'loopholes', but they are simply a way for passengers to bring some sanity to the many situations where the ticketing system lets them down. The problem is that while train operating companies' websites have to show the cheapest *ticket* for their journey, they take this too literally, when it is clear that a combination of *tickets* would be the preferred option for the vast majority of passengers, given that it would present no additional restrictions on when and where they could travel. Despite repeated criticism from passenger groups and politicians, the train operators have done little to improve public awareness.[23]

Another example of this is the 'excess' rule, which allows passengers to pay the difference between two ticket types in the event of a change in travel plans, which is usually cheaper than buying a new ticket altogether. Take, for example, the case of my tablemate Sam. He holds an off-peak return from London to Stockport costing £94, which he will use to return to London tomorrow. But what if his plans change, and instead he wants to carry on past Stockport to Manchester Piccadilly, returning from Manchester to London the next day? Most passengers would assume this needs an extra ticket. Were Sam to log onto his app to purchase one, he would be led to believe that, because returns are not valid between Stockport and Manchester for longer than a day, he would need to buy a single from Stockport to Manchester today, and a single from Manchester to Stockport tomorrow, for a combined price of £8.60 – a lot of money for only a short extension to his journey. But what Sam should actually do is ask the guard to 'excess' his ticket. This would allow him to only pay the difference in cost between his London–Stockport return and a London–Manchester return, which is only 50p, so saving him £8.10.

Excess tickets attract zero publicity. For example, they are not mentioned at all on the government-owned National Rail website, which is supposed to be the main port of call for passengers seeking impartial ticket and travel information. To get information on these types of ticket, which even railway staff sometimes have little knowledge of, passengers must resort to online information shared between members of the public, for example through the Rail UK Forum Fares and Ticketing Guide.[24]

It seems as if the train operating companies and the government do not want to advertise split tickets and excess fares because it would lose the railways income and increase subsidy. In other words, they are happy to cite seldom-available 'bargain' fares, such as advances, to distract political attention from huge walk-up fares, but are completely shtum about legitimate ways to make those walk-up fares more affordable.

Beware the ticket police

At the same as fares have become more complex and more expensive, efforts by rail companies to clamp down on 'fare evasion' have increased. Train operating companies have outsourced the processing of penalty fares (fines) to third-party debt collectors, who use scare tactics familiar to anyone who has been chased for debt – threats of bad credit ratings, court action and criminal records. As investigations by watchdog Passenger Focus have shown, train operating companies, and the organisations they hire to 'recover' funds, often fail to take a common-sense approach to passengers travelling with the wrong documentation and are quick to escalate cases towards prosecution.[25]

Among many examples of over-zealous 'revenue protection' detailed in reports by Passenger Focus and newspapers are the following:

A passenger was penalised for changing trains at Portsmouth Harbour rather than Fratton (as per his ticket) for a connection to Fareham. His existing ticket was confiscated, forcing him to buy another, and he was issued a penalty fare.[26]

A child was caught travelling in the wrong zones. He was charged a penalty fare despite the fact that the ticket he had bought and the ticket he should have bought were exactly the same price – there was no revenue loss whatsoever to the company. The mother complained only to be told 'rules are rules'.[27]

Newspapers also report passengers being penalised for getting off their train one or two stops early.[28] Such is the complexity of the ticketing system that lack of awareness by staff can even lead to prosecutions outside the letter of the law:

A passenger had a valid ticket for her journey. The guard wrongly felt that it was invalid and issued an Unpaid Fare Notice (for £154) on the grounds of her having 'no ticket'.[29]

In this case, it was only after a third round of appeal, under the threat of immediate criminal prosecution, that the debt collectors backed down.

Of course, in practice many passengers are given the benefit of the doubt. Rail staff can use discretion, and often do. But that doesn't stop many passengers who have made innocent mistakes from being caught in the penalty fare net. Dealing with passengers in this harsh and legalistic way maximises the railways' income. Or it *appears* to – in fact, railways are undoubtedly losing income in the longer term, by making passengers' experience much more difficult and stressful than it needs to be.

Beware fare 'reform'

In 2018, with support from the government, the train operating companies' trade body, the Rail Delivery Group, launched a review of ticketing, with the aim of simplifying the fares structure. The organisation conducted a high-profile consultation campaign, asking passengers and organisations to comment on its fare reform proposals. This generated an impressive total of 19,000 responses.[30] Unsurprisingly, it found that passengers agreed that the fare system needed simplifying, and also wanted lower fares. They propose, for example, ending the situation where passengers must pay for peak fares even where one leg of the journey is entirely off-peak, and ending situations where it is cheaper to split tickets. This could indeed reduce the cost of some journeys, which sounds good until you see the small print.

One of the reasons our train is packed to the rafters is that it's the first off-peak service leaving Euston. Every weekday the 18:34 departure is virtually empty and the 18:57 is packed out, because the first is in the peak (meaning that a single to Manchester costs £184.70) and the second is not (£66.10). Only those on lucrative business expense accounts won't wait the extra twenty-three minutes to save the best part of £120. In the Rail Delivery Group's proposals, instead of this 'cliff edge' between peak and off-peak trains, there would be something like a sliding scale, with the least busy peak trains being cheaper than they are now.

However, the proposals come with an important caveat: all reforms must be 'revenue neutral'.[31] This means that any savings that some passengers experience must be made up for by increased costs to other passengers. That would make the busiest off-peak services more expensive, which would *limit* choice. Taking the Euston example again, it would increase the cost of the 18:57 – a terrible development for lower-income passengers, for whom the walk-up off-peak fare is already barely affordable but is the only realistic way to reach London from Manchester on a weekday day trip. In other words, it would probably decrease fares for wealthier business travellers and increase fares for the vast majority when they most need to travel.

Because the Rail Delivery Group is the trade body of the train operating companies and government-owned Network Rail, it is not surprising that it wants to do away with what it sees as commercially onerous regulations, which put pressure on corporate profits and public finances. It's not fare regulation which has caused passengers the most grief, as the Rail Delivery Group deceitfully implies. As we have seen, fare regulation was implemented at privatisation to ease passengers' concerns that private companies would put profit before people. In reality, successive governments have used regulation to shift the costs of the railways onto passengers. Any reform of fares needs to redress that.

It didn't have to be this way

Increased industry costs – the case of the rolling stock

The Rail Delivery Group justifies high fares by claiming that '98p in every pound from fares goes back into running and maintaining the railway'. That figure includes the cost of 'staff', 'train leasing', 'track and infrastructure', 'payments to government', 'fuel and energy' and 'other', including 'track maintenance'. Only 2p in every pound is therefore taken as 'profit'.[32] This sounds entirely reasonable. Passengers want to know that, even if fares are higher than they want, nearly all the money they're paying goes towards running and improving the railways, not being squirreled away by shareholders. But on closer inspection, the Rail Delivery Group's figures show nothing of the sort. That's because they refer solely to the train operating companies' finances.[33] It's true that the train operating companies have low profit margins as a proportion of their income, somewhere around 2p to 5p in every pound they receive.[34] But they are unusual businesses, in that they own very little capital. They hire both track space and rolling stock to run services. So although their profit margins seem low, they are in fact very high in view of the lack of investment they make in the railways.[35] When the Rail Delivery Group says that much of the price of a ticket is for the costs of tracks and infrastructure, it neglects to mention the outsourcing of infrastructure work to private contractors and the private financing arrangements used by Network Rail, both of which have sucked vast quantities of money from the rail system.[36] These aspects of private wealth extraction from the railways were described in Chapter 1.

Also pushing up the cost of providing rail services, and therefore the price of tickets, has been the private provision of rolling stock. Under BR, the majority of rolling stock was owned, and often built, by BR itself.[37] Rolling stock production and use were therefore conducted mostly on a not-for-profit basis: BR paid what it cost to build and maintain the trains, and little more. Privatisation saw BR's rolling stock split into three batches, then sold whole to private investors. The three private rolling stock companies were supposed to compete with each other in providing rolling stock to the train operating companies. Like the other aspects of rail privatisation, this was supposed to save the government money. It was thought competition would incentivise the rolling stock companies to improve maintenance efficiency and provide private finance to build new trains.

Yet true competition never really happened. In reality, rolling stock is not easily interchangeable. Trains are usually made to order, for work on particular routes and for particular types of service. Electric trains designed for intercity journeys are entirely unsuitable for stopping services on unelectrified rural lines. The kind of competition the privatisers envisaged would rely on a certain amount of spare capacity in the rolling stock market, and otherwise train operating companies would mostly be stuck with the stock they already used. But, thanks to increased demand for rail travel, there were few spare sets to be found. Rolling stock companies were supposed to be incentivised to invest in new stock. But they found that it was usually more profitable to keep hold of their existing stock than to go for major new procurement. It took government bans of unsafe and outdated stock for any serious investment to occur, but never at a level to create proper competition.[38]

This led to some horrendous overcharging. Contracts between rolling stock and train operating companies are largely kept secret, with public disclosure barred because of 'commercial confidentiality'.[39] But occasionally information seeps through. For example, it was reported in 2006 that a two-carriage pacer train, which had been built by BR in the 1980s and had originally cost £700,000 to construct, was attracting an annual leasing charge of £106,000.[40]

The three rolling stock companies remain, having been bought and sold between various banks and international financial investment firms. And, although there have been some new entrants to the market, trains owned by the three original rolling stock companies still account for around 87 per cent of the national fleet.[41] A recent investigation found that, in the six years to 2018, the 'big three' passed a combined total of £1.2 billion to their parent companies and owners. All of the big three companies are formed by complex networks of shell companies which span international borders, some of which are based in tax havens. Those shell companies make loans and interest payments to each other in a way that makes public scrutiny of their finances difficult, but it is very likely that they are deliberately designed to avoid standard UK corporate tax rates.[42] This is money that could be used to reduce fares.

Lack of competition and 'tax efficiency' came about because the Major government made the disastrous decision not to regulate the rolling stock companies at privatisation. After the railways' financial catastrophe after the Hatfield crash, Tony Blair's government lost patience and asked the Competition Commission to investigate the rolling stock companies for overcharging. The commission agreed that there was little competition in the 'market'.[43] Despite this, it rejected regulation, claiming that it would have 'distorting effects on the market' – in other words that it would deter private investment in the industry.[44] A stable 'regulatory environment' is judged to be a 'credit strength' by those responsible for assessing rolling stock companies' creditworthiness.[45] In other words, having very little regulation improves rolling stock companies' profit rates, because it lowers their cost of accessing finance; any increase in that cost would make the rolling stock companies financially unviable in the eyes of investors.

If regulation is out of the question, then the obvious solution would be to circumvent the rolling stock companies altogether by re-establishing public manufacturing and supply. By the mid-2000s, much of the stock owned by the rolling stock companies, which they inherited from BR, was becoming obsolete. A publicly owned rolling stock company could have supplied new trains from that point, gradually diminishing the private rolling stock companies' market stranglehold as their trains became obsolete. But this option was apparently never considered. A candid statement by an investment bank advising the government at the time gives a clue as to why, claiming that the difficulty for the government 'was that it wanted better value for taxpayers, but it did not want to have the rolling stock on its balance sheet'.[46]

Renationalising rolling stock provision would have caused the government short-term financial hardship for long-term financial gain. Instead of doing anything to rein in the rolling stock companies, New Labour left them unregulated, with no alternative public provision, and successive governments have done the same.[47] This has left the railways with much higher costs than necessary, although their exact extent remains hidden from public view, and these have been passed on to passengers through ever more expensive fares. But the option of not-for-profit public procurement is always there.

The great British motoring subsidy

Creating a publicly owned railway system is a prerequisite for substantially reducing fares. However, thanks to years of failed privatisation experiments, governments will face massive subsidy bills for years to come, and these will always discourage them from making rail travel more affordable. But when railways are considered part of a larger transport system, that dynamic needs to be questioned. In the past twenty years, at the same time as jacking up rail fares, governments have made motoring much cheaper.

In 1993, the Tory chancellor Norman Lamont introduced a motor fuel duty 'escalator'. Its purpose was to reduce the UK's carbon dioxide emissions, following the its commitments made at the 1992 United Nations Earth Summit, at which global leaders agreed that measures were needed to mitigate the effects of climate change. Initially set at a 3 per cent increase above inflation every year, by the end of Tory rule the annual increase in fuel duty was raised to 5 per cent. Coming to power in 1997, Tony Blair's government – impressed by the escalator's apparent success in reducing emissions, and seeing it as an important part of its own sustainable transport ambitions – then raised it to a 6 per cent annual increase above inflation.[48] However, the escalator was abandoned by Gordon Brown in 1999, bending to criticisms that higher duties hurt the country's international competitiveness and people who had no public transport alternative. The move was given a cautious welcome by motoring organisations. As a sop to environmentalists, the government committed itself to ring-fencing money raised through fuel duty for spending on public transport.[49]

Despite Brown's generosity to motorists, a protest movement led by road hauliers and farmers blockaded the country's fuel supply. Although duty had been frozen, prices were much higher than usual, thanks to a combination of a high oil price and the effect of accumulated increases in duty rates over previous years. The blockades led to massive fuel shortages and panic buying. Despite considerable efforts to break the blockades, Blair and Brown eventually caved in, promising fuel duty cuts of between 2p and 3p per litre below current rates.[50]

The fuel protests effectively marked the end of governments' use of the tax system to discourage car use in order to mitigate climate change, while the idea that fuel tax could be ring-fenced for public transport was quickly and quietly dropped.[51] The result has been real-terms cuts to fuel duty almost every year since 1999 (see Figure 2.3). According to the Institute for Fiscal Studies, fuel duty cuts have led to a fall of £19 billion a year in government income, in today's values.[52] As a result, motor fuel consumption

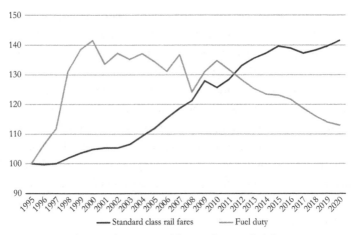

Figure 2.3 Real-terms changes in rail fares and motor fuel duty, 1995–2020.

remains at a level similar to that when the fuel duty escalator was introduced,[53] despite increases in engine efficiency. That is because of year-on-year increases in the use of motor vehicles, which have resulted in a 19 per cent increase in car miles driven from 2000 to 2019.[54]

The early 2000s were a fork in the road for transport policy. A decade after world governments agreed to cooperate to combat 'dangerous human interference with the climate system,'[55] and with transport-created air pollution high up the agenda,[56] the New Labour government decided, almost simultaneously, to make train travel much more expensive, and motoring much cheaper (see Figure 2.3). These decisions have been effectively ratified by every successive government. The amount of tax income lost every year as a result of cuts to fuel duty is almost double the railways' annual income from fares. In fact, it is more than the total passenger income of the rail and bus industries combined. In other words, for the same money, *public transport could have been made free.*

Instead, the car industry was promoted,[57] to the severe detriment of the environment and those on the lowest incomes.[58]

That successive governments of different stripes have continued this great motoring subsidy is testament to the political power of the car industry and the continued popularity of driving. Rail fares are so high because successive governments have refused to fund railways properly, but also because they have been too politically weak to try to stem decades of increasing motoring. This had led to the carless – around 25 per cent of all households – having to pay high public transport fares in order to avoid (often only slightly higher) car running costs,[59] while the environmental problems that cars cause – already well apparent by the early 1990s – have grown into a desperate emergency.

Conclusion

According to mainstream economics, free markets are the most efficient means of allocating society's resources. Resources are scarce, and the most efficient way to distribute them is through the price system, which reflects supply and demand. But most economists acknowledge that, in practice, there are limits to what free markets can achieve. The existence of 'natural monopolies' in some sectors means that competitive struggle between entrepreneurs is impossible without collapse of that sector. In the language of economics, natural monopolies cause 'market failure' – which means that state has to get involved in some way to ensure that essential goods and services are provided. Railways are a good example of this, and that's why they have generally been either state-run or heavily regulated by the state.

Another form of market failure is the creation of externalities. These are situations where the costs or benefits of an economic activity are not reflected in prices. A good example is contemporary car use. Motoring is cheap for the individual, but very expensive for society because of its environmental destruction. Conversely, transport modes that are much better for the environment, like buses and trains, are very expensive for individual users. Without government intervention to redress the balance, poorer transport users who cannot afford to drive are burdened with a disproportionately high allocation of the costs of collective environmental responsibility.

Despite the ideology of customer choice that accompanied privatisation, Sam's ticket is so expensive because governments have decided it should be. They've decided that Sam should be a loser, while railway companies' shareholders, the car industry and those on the highest incomes who have benefited from tax cuts should be winners.[60] Transport is highly political, always involving struggle over who our transport systems serve and who pays for both the service it provides and its environmental impacts. As we will see in the following chapters, that struggle is far from over.

3

Why are there so many strikes?

It is 22:30 and we are stuck again. A rumour is circulating that the reason for the delay is a signal failure ahead, so no trains are passing through. Ruth reports that train companies are advising people on Twitter 'not to travel'. Little use for those of us already on the tracks. The still, inky blackness outside the carriage evokes the feeling of being cast adrift in the middle of a calm ocean, not, as we are, stranded five miles south of Stafford.

The news wakes Sam, who has long been slumbering in that restless purgatory between wakefulness and sleep.

'The thing is', he offers, slowly, 'I get what you're saying about privatisation – it hasn't worked. But half the time, it's not the train company that's made me late, but the unions. The amount of times I've sat for hours on a replacement bus when the union's called another bloody strike. You won't fix the railways without sorting out the unions. We all want a pay rise, but it's getting ridiculous.'

Ruth agrees. She works part-time in Manchester city centre in retail. Her journey to work has been hit by strike action, leading to constant stress and arguments with her line managers.

You can understand their frustration. They, like millions of others, are on insecure contracts. Being late is not just an inconvenience – it can mean the difference between keeping and losing a job.

Anyone familiar with rail strikes will know that they are accompanied by an unsightly slanging match between union leaders and rail company managers. The two groups are trying to compete for public sympathy, to blame the other side for the full sidings and empty platforms. Union leaders complain of greedy, money-grabbing bosses. In turn, they are portrayed as 'union barons' holding the public to ransom. This makes for good headlines and clickbait, but does little to inform the public about why strikes happen and what is at stake.

Ruth's regular commute is from Walkden, in Salford's suburbs, to Manchester – a route that has been heavily disrupted by strikes. In total, forty-seven days of strike action were recently taken by Northern Rail staff over the course of a year.[1] What would motivate any group of workers to take such sustained strike action? After all, striking is a risky business: there are no guarantees of winning, you may be disciplined by management for taking part, and each day you are on strike is a day's pay lost.

The strike related to the attempted removal of 'guards' (otherwise known as 'conductors' and 'train managers') by Northern. Among guards' most important responsibilities are the closing of doors to ensure a safe departure from stations, the checking of tickets and interacting with passengers. Northern, alongside other train operating companies, claims that it is no longer necessary for guards to perform the first of these duties. With new technology such as strategically placed cameras, the driver can dispatch the train safely, leaving the guard free to pay more attention to customers.

The union representing guards, the RMT, knew very well that taking away the responsibility of door closure and dispatch was really a plan to cut guards from services in order to save money. The government played its usual role of standing above the dispute. The regional transport body Transport for the North urged both sides to get around the negotiating table.[2] In fact, the staff cuts were part of Northern's franchise contract with the government. Effectively, it had to cut staff or risk being financially penalised. What is more, train operating companies are fully compensated for lost income in the event of a strike. In other words, it is government policy to remove guards from trains. The strike was therefore, in reality, against the government, not Northern.

Looked at this way, the attempted removal of guards, and the strikes that it has provoked, are simply another consequence of the railways' financial crisis. However, an understanding of the development of the railways over the past two decades reveals that attempts to save money by attacking rail workers is not a new phenomenon. In fact, this objective – even though it was never officially admitted – was at the heart of the privatisation project from the very beginning.

The politics of how railway workers have been treated by their employers, and their reaction to that treatment through collective activity in trade unions, have played an important role in the railways' development. The fact that the railways are a loss-making industry creates a considerable incentive for the funders – central government – to cut staffing costs to the bone. Many of the jobs performed on the railways require specialist, industry-specific skills: driving a train does not qualify you to take the wheel of a bus, and it would be foolish to let a signaller loose in air traffic control. Many railway workers cannot easily shift employer to seek better wages or working conditions – a position that railway managers have the potential to exploit.

However, the same constraints on rail workers moving outside the industry also make it difficult to replace them, giving rail workers more *potential power* than workers in many other industries. Although railways are loss-making, they are vital to keep society functioning. As Sam knows all too well, when railway workers take strike action, the economic effects are felt far beyond the industry. To take one example, it was estimated that the impact of twenty-seven days of strike action on one franchise resulted in a £300 million reduction in national economic output.[3]

The greedy unions and their 'direct line to the taxpayer'

A major motivation for the privatisation programme by Conservative governments in the 1980s and 1990s was the desire to reform the labour relations of the public enterprises. Nationalised industries were thought to be prone to 'producer capture' by unions, which put their own interests ahead of the industries' customers.[4] Workers' wages were inflated by unions' national pay bargaining, underpinned by their ability to bring entire industries to a halt. Selfish workers were aided and abetted by supine managers more interested in keeping the peace than in keeping costs low, or so the argument went.

The Conservative governments' solution to this was to privatise and fragment the nationalised industries. It was thought that if these industries were in the private sector, managers would be pressurised by shareholders to save money on staffing. If privatisation created competition between companies, it would sharpen managers' resolve to bear down on wages. If it could fragment monopolies, it would destroy collective bargaining by eroding the ability of unions to organise across industries. It was exactly this thinking which informed rail privatisation.[5]

The passenger service franchising system was designed to cut labour costs. As explained in Chapter 2, given that many of train operating companies' costs are fixed – such as the costs of using the infrastructure and hiring rolling stock – it is largely through reducing spending on staff, which makes up only 29 per cent of their total operating expenditure,[6] that bidders for franchises hope to find a cutting edge over their rivals.

In the early years of privatisation, the train operating companies duly attempted to bring down labour costs by cutting staff. However, cutting staff merely led to staff shortages. Shortages became especially acute as demand for services grew in the late 1990s, which led to train companies laying on extra services, requiring more staff. In the first six years of privatisation, the number of staff employed by train operating companies increased by 11 per cent.[7] The experience suggests that there was little slack to cut from the workforce that had been inherited from BR.[8]

The railways' post-Hatfield financial crisis, and the restructuring that it caused, heralded a fresh wave of commentary on the privatised system and its control of costs. This included renewed criticisms of the privatised system and arguments for renationalisation,[9] but also calls for *more* competition as a way to solve the railways' financial crisis – for the government to get out of the way and stop 'meddling'.[10]

Prominent among the latter group of commentators was Professor Stephen Glaister. Glaister is an expert in transport policy and regulation, having been an economic adviser to BR and, later, the Rail Regulator. His 1993 pamphlet for the Institute of Economic Affairs, a free market think tank, gave critical support to the government's rail privatisation plans.[11] In 2004 he revisited the subject of railway economics in a new publication. He argued that the railways' financial problems had been a result of government interference in the competitive system established through privatisation. There are different ways railways can run successfully, but if competition is a policy objective, then it cannot work if governments bail out private firms, as had been done with Railtrack and on numerous occasions with train operating companies.[12]

For Glaister, government interference had prevented the 'single most effective efficiency gain' that privatisation could have brought: a 'competitive market for labour'.[13] Glaister argued that rail workers had fared better than their counterparts in other privatised industries, with the bus industry serving as a useful comparison. Buses were privatised in 1985, allowing unfettered competition between bus operators. New operators sprang to life and began to aggressively compete with the newly privatised municipal bus companies. This created intense competition for a dwindling number of passengers, leading to 'bus wars' characterised by queues of mostly empty buses, clogging up Britain's towns and cities.[14] Competition was waged largely on the basis of how far bus companies could reduce staffing costs.[15]

As Glaister argues, as a result of privatisation,

> If a bus company runs into financial difficulty with a route it will quickly withdraw and the route may or may not be taken over by a competing company. In short, the forces of competition are effective at punishing attempts to extract returns to labour or capital over and above the going competitive rate. Jobs are genuinely at risk.[16]

Intense competition within a market significantly reduces the profitability of competing companies. Low profit rates reduce the scope to offer the workers wage rises. If workers from one company strike for significantly better wages than the industry standard, they are much more likely to find themselves out of a job than receiving a pay rise, because that would make their employer unprofitable.[17] It was through an intensively competitive market, Glaister argues, that the privatised bus companies were able to reduce costs by as much as 40 per cent.

This contrasts greatly with the situation of the privatised railways, where competitive forces are nowhere near as strong, thanks to the government's commitment to bail out failing companies. According to Glaister, 'those who negotiate on behalf of labour' – the unions – 'know this. They sense that at the end of the day they have a direct line to the taxpayer and that they are in a strong bargaining position.'[18]

Indeed, private bus companies like Stagecoach, First, National Express and Go-Ahead had 'success' in reducing costs in their own industries, primarily through the reduction of labour costs. This motivated them to move quickly into rail franchising and to attempt a similar strategy there.[19] However, the same companies were nowhere near as 'successful' in the rail industry, and Glaister's argument is correct in the sense that one of the reasons for that has been the political impossibility of letting rail services die, as many bus services unfortunately have.[20] But his analysis is flawed in important ways: he exaggerates rail unions' success at improving pay and conditions since privatisation, he glosses over the very different levels of 'structural power' that different kinds of rail worker possess, and he ignores the importance of subjective factors, such as the quality of union organisation and the determination of workers to win. These points will now be taken in turn.

Rail workers' pay and conditions: the reality

The average pay for a railway worker has barely changed since privatisation. Although of course there has been some fluctuation, the average rail worker earns about the same today as twenty years ago. Although there are some gaps in the data, it is clear that the overall picture is neither of excessive pay rises nor of excessive pay cuts (see Figure 3.1).[21] However, the average hides important differences in the fates of different types of railway worker, which to a large extent have depended on their skill level and position within the railway system.

Railtrack was incentivised by its shareholders to reduce mainte-nance costs as much as possible. As Sir Christopher Foster, one of the chief architects of rail privatisation, explained, in the provision of infrastructure 'the efficiency gains will largely ... be in the use of people so as to achieve higher standards at lower costs'.[22] Much rail-way maintenance work is highly labour-intensive. This means that the only realistic way to cut costs in order to remain competitive is to attempt to reduce pay to railway workers, by either minimising the workforce or paying workers less. Health and safety protocols

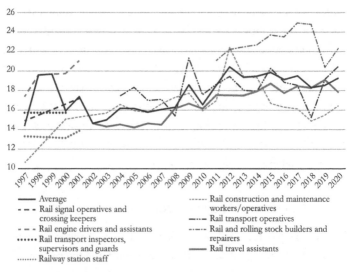

Figure 3.1 Real-terms pay of railway workers since privatisation, 1997–2020, £ per hour.

went out of the window as workers found themselves often working in unfamiliar roles and places, on insecure contracts and in dangerous conditions. The terrible personal consequences for track workers were brilliantly portrayed in Ken Loach's film *The Navigators*.[23]

Taken together, the steadily declining pay for rail maintenance workers since the mid-2000s and the continued lack of job security are testament to privatisation's 'success' in undermining the livelihoods of infrastructure workers. That trend has been somewhat mitigated by the bringing in house of Network Rail maintenance workers after Railtrack's collapse, but zero-hours contracts and use of agency workers remain rife in rail infrastructural work, and there is a long way to go in order to bring health and safety up to the standard expected by the safety inspectorate.[24]

Although railway maintenance involves highly specialised skills, much of the labour is performed by relatively unskilled workers, meaning that they can be easily replaced. Outsourcing, and the terrible pay and conditions it creates, are also ubiquitous in numerous ancillary roles, like those of cleaners, caterers and security staff. At the other extreme are train drivers, whose training period of up to twelve months far exceeds that of other operational railway staff.[25] To train a train driver is very expensive, as argued in Chapter 1. Given train operating companies' focus on short-term profitability, they find undertaking this expenditure less appealing than 'poaching' drivers from other companies. The result is a long-term under-supply of drivers,[26] a situation that the drivers' union ASLEF has skilfully exploited to significantly raise drivers' pay since privatisation.[27]

We can see from these examples that rail workers' ability to increase their wages depends to a significant extent on their 'structural power'. One of the principal factors in structural power is the tightness of the labour markets created by the skill levels required of workers.[28] Longer training periods and higher training costs tend to make for tighter labour markets, as is the case with train drivers. The tighter the labour market, the less easy it is to break strikes by sacking unruly workers and replacing them with compliant ones.

As the next section will demonstrate, guards fall somewhere between the extremes of the low and high skill levels of track workers and drivers respectively. The guards' strike also illustrates well the importance of the subjective factors which determine workers' pay and job security, such as the quality of union organisation and the determination of strikers.[29]

The guards' strike

The failure of New Labour to arrest the rise in railway costs following its post-Hatfield reforms led to a search for 'value for money' by the Tory prime minister David Cameron's government. The resulting 'McNulty report' made a series of recommendations relating to the regulation of the railway system. The report brought about little in the way of policy change, except in one crucial respect: its insistence that savings of £256 million a year could be made through taking advantage of 'significant opportunities to achieve improved value for money in the people area'.[30]

Central to the proposals was the widespread introduction of 'driver-only operation' (DOO) – operation of trains without a guard. The report stated:

The financial imperatives facing the industry, the need to change radically the cost structure of the industry, and the availability of new communications technology has led the Study to recommend that the default position for all services on the GB rail network should be DOO with a second member of train crew only being provided where there is a commercial, technical or other imperative.[31]

The McNulty report presaged a war between the government and railway workers. The strikes that it provoked were to last over four years – the most prolonged series of strikes in the railways' history, causing massive disruption to rail services and inflicting huge damage on the economy. It cost the government hundreds of millions of pounds to compensate the train operating companies for the lost income that the strikes created.[32] But although it managed to inflict some causalities on the other side, this was a war that the government lost.

The first skirmishes broke out in 2016 on Southern rail services, operated by Govia Thameslink Railway (GTR). GTR proposed to re-classify guards as 'on board supervisors' – second staff members but with many of the traditional safety responsibilities removed, including the dispatch of trains from stations, which would pass to drivers. GTR claimed that removing these responsibilities would allow staff more time to check tickets and help customers. The drivers' union ASELF and the guards' union the RMT saw the proposed changes as a naked attempt to introduce widespread driver-only operation in order to cut costs. For its part, GTR argued that although giving drivers more safety responsibilities meant that it could *technically* run services without second staff members, it had no intention of doing so, except in 'exceptional circumstances'. In that case, it would be better to run a train with just a driver than cancel the service altogether, which had been the only option up to now. The unions' scepticism about that argument can be understood. GTR refused to define what it meant by 'exceptional circumstances'. Indeed, thanks to systematic under-staffing, staff shortages were a *daily* occurrence – did they count as 'exceptional'?[33] Moreover, it was public knowledge that the government, in line with the McNulty recommendations, had *specified* the roll-out of driver-only operation in the tendering process that led to GTR taking over services in 2014.[34]

The political stakes of the strike were made clear in February 2016 in a public meeting in Croydon – one of the major calling points for Southern services – hosted by then MP and Tory government minister Gavin Barwell. Barwell had invited along Peter Wilkinson, a senior official in the Department for Transport. Wilkinson's comments at that meeting have become the stuff of railway folklore. On addressing the unions' response to GTR's imposition of driver-only operation, Wilkinson advised the audience that 'over the next three years we're going to be having punch-ups and we will see industrial action and I want your support'. Wilkinson's tone suggested that the government's long-term objective was to dismantle union power once and for all. 'We have got to break them', he added. 'They can't afford to spend too long on strike and I will push them into that place. They will have to decide if they want to give a good service or get the hell out of my industry.'[35]

Wilkinson later apologised for his remarks, but his call to arms was nonetheless taken seriously by union leaderships. The RMT realised that taking the responsibility away from guards for the control of doors did not only have important safety implications; it would also weaken the union in the longer term. What leverage would the guards have if trains could run without them needing to be present to operate the doors? A strike would simply be another 'exceptional circumstance' – trains would continue to run without them, and the strike would be crushed.

The Southern strike began with two days of strike action by guards in April 2016.[36] They were joined by drivers later in 2016, greatly increasing the overall impact of the strike.[37] Drivers too were angry at the potential loss of guards, which would mean adding extra safety responsibilities to an already demanding and safety critical role. However, in November 2017 drivers voted to accept a 28.5 per cent pay increase over the next five years in return for ending their dispute with GTR, following the recommendation of the ASLEF leadership.[38] Such a high pay increase for manual workers is rare in post-Thatcher Britain. It further exemplified the lengths the government was determined to go to in order to test the resolve of guards and the RMT. It was also an unfortunate example of how it is easier for management to employ divide-and-rule tactics when workers belong to more than one union.[39]

Because they were unable to coordinate strikes with the backing of the drivers, the guards' ability to disrupt services was severely curtailed. It did not help that some driver-only-operated trains were already operating on the same routes – a legacy of cost-cutting by BR in the 1980s.[40] The RMT pledged to continue the strike. However, the weakness of the guards' position led them to signing contracts to become 'on board supervisors', effectively ending the strike.

Although the RMT lost the GTR battle, the war between guards and the government, on the national scale, had only just begun. It was to eventually encompass strikes across eight different franchises, which together totalled 153 strike days over four years,[41] involving some 8,000 guards.[42] Each dispute on each franchise counted as a legally separate dispute. Some disputes were settled early, with the train operating company providing swift assurances on the continued use of guards, for example on Greater Anglia (eight days) and West Midlands Trains (three days). Disputes on other franchises lasted much longer, for example the twenty-seven days of strikes on South-West Trains and the mammoth forty-seven days of strikes on Northern. The disruption to services was greater than these figures suggest because a strike on one day also affects the next day's services. Striking was supplemented by additional action, not least overtime bans. These were a particularly effective form of action because, thanks to years of attempts to cut costs, train operating companies rely on staff working overtime as a matter of course.

The guards were up against substantial obstacles. One was lost pay. While to some extent this can be made up by the union's own funds, those funds are limited. Anyone striking for forty-seven days will face a significant loss of income. The temptation to cross the picket lines with a mortgage to pay and mouths to feed is strong. Another obstacle was the use of managers to guard trains. This was a tactic which the RMT questioned on safety grounds because managers did not necessarily have the requisite skills and experience to guard trains safely. Indeed, their use by one train operating company was banned by the railway inspectorate following an investigation.[43] Another significant difficulty for the RMT in taking action is the presence of some of the most restrictive anti-union laws in the world, which complicate the organisation of strikes with legal hurdles and limit the scope and duration of strikes. Train companies launched a number of unsuccessful, but nevertheless disruptive, attempts to overthrow strike ballots at the High Court. Finally, the strikes occurred in a context of decades of very low levels of strike activity and trade union membership, thereby limiting potential solidarity and support from other unions.

The guards thus faced considerable obstacles to winning the war. However, although the RMT lost the Southern dispute, agreements have since been reached to retain guards on Northern,[44] Greater Anglia,[45] Merseyrail,[46] ScotRail,[47] East Coast,[48] and West Midlands Trains,[49] while, at the time of writing, the outcome of the dispute on South Western is still to be resolved.[50] Although the rail companies' threat of driver-only operation has not gone away (it seems to rear its ugly head every time a franchise is re-contracted), these agreements represent a position far from the widespread roll-out of driver-only operation envisaged in the McNulty report, and a poor return for the extra public spending and economic damage that the government has been willing to tolerate. So why, given the obstacles the guards were up against, can the RMT claim to have 'successfully pushed back' its opponents on franchise after franchise?[51]

Superficial analysis of the RMT likens it to the defunct militant trade unions in the nationalised industries of the 1970s and 1980s. But that ignores the transformation of the union since privatisation. That transformation was spearheaded by the (now deceased) former general secretary Bob Crow, who still looms over the organisation, politically and culturally. Crow was a pantomime villain of the press, derided as, among many other things, a 'canteen demagogue',[52] a 'dinosaur'[53] and a 'left-wing agitator straight out of the *I'm All Right Jack* school of Neanderthal militancy'.[54] Even critics of rail privatisation policy took issue with his supposedly outdated approach to disputes.[55] For example, Christian Wolmar commented that the RMT's constant threat of strikes meant that 'that the last thing any government would want to do is to give his union more power by bringing transport more into the public fold'.[56]

Crow was elected as general secretary of the RMT in 2002. He was part of a left-wing platform which was critical of the previous leadership's failure to mount a serious challenge to rail privatisation. The group aimed to turn the RMT into a more democratic organisation and one that was more willing to take the fight to the employers.[57] The fragmentation of collective bargaining posed considerable problems for the RMT. It meant that the union had to recruit negotiators, who would act on a regional, rather than national, level.[58] The leadership's desire to improve union democracy combined with the need to organise on a more local level to strengthen the participation and voice of ordinary members. Increased participation made strikes (and the more frequent *threat* of strikes) more powerful. Winning disputes increased membership still further, arresting the years of decline in membership under the previous leadership.[59]

In other words, far from being stuck in the past, Crow's leadership was a decisive *break* from the top-down and more moderate style that had characterised rail trade unionism in the latter years of BR. Privatisation had severely disrupted rail unions' ability to organise, as was intended. However, it also allowed the RMT to create localised democratic structures through which rail workers could organise to fight against the erosions of their working conditions and damage to the industry that privatisation created.

Overall, contrary to Glaister's argument, the impact of privatisation on the ability of rail workers to defend themselves from attacks on their pay and conditions of employment has been very uneven, but few can claim to have done well out of it. Privatisation was a disaster for many workers, and can be said to have clearly benefited only drivers, thanks to the particular structural position it put them in. Most rail workers do not enjoy such advantages. The extent to which some grades, such as guards, have been able to maintain their job security and pay is to a great extent a result of both the quality of their collective organisation and their determination to overcome the considerable obstacles they have faced to make strikes successful. The guards' strike is a stark example to those in other industries that privatisation does not have to result in the pay cuts and job losses it is designed to create.

Access denied

A myopic focus on cutting staffing costs can also easily obscure the benefits that rail workers bring to passengers. Although it may be technically possible to run trains with only one member of staff, is it even desirable? Railways were not designed with level access from platforms to trains, which means that wheelchair users cannot board trains without a ramp and the assistance of a member of staff. Ideally, station staff would provide assistance, but staffing at stations has been reduced in recent years, also thanks to cost-cutting in the wake of the McNulty report: only 17 per cent of stations are staffed all day, and 45 per cent are completely unstaffed.[60] If station staff are not present, help needs to be provided by a second staff member, a role which does not exist under driver-only operation.

The Disabled Persons Transport Advisory Committee has warned of the potential for discriminatory behaviour towards disabled passengers resulting from a 'toxic combination' consisting of 'driver-only operation, when combined with unstaffed stations'.[61] Rail companies claim that disabled passengers can ensure that they will be able to board by booking assistance.[62] But this must be done twenty-four hours in advance, while non-disabled passengers can just turn up and go. As a report commissioned by the Association of Train Operating Companies warned in 2015, the planned extension of driver-only operation 'does have significant accessibility implications'. It continued: 'Given the growing number of older passengers and the clear evidence of their need for the presence of staff both for reassurance and for assistance, it is hard to see how these further economies meets this imperative.' Furthermore, 'it is difficult too, in legal terms, to see how trains with no staff to provide assistance running through unstaffed stations cannot come under the heading of a "provision, criterion or practice" that discriminates. (Section 20 of the Equality Act 2010).' As a consequence, 'it is Conductors [guards] who are best placed to ensure that assistance is delivered effectively and in accordance with the law'.[63]

Indeed, as can be seen in a statement by a guard describing a typical day, the range of accessibility duties they perform is extensive: 'Assisting on [and] off [the] train at unmanned stations. Helping with communications, arranging onward assistance. Reassuring vulnerable adults. [Helping] children with Autism [and] communications [disabilities]. Assisting blind [and] deaf passengers etc.'[64]

There is evidence that the extension of driver-only operation on Southern has already reduced the accessibility of services. In its own investigation into the impact of implementing the practice on Southern, GTR claimed that forty-eight disabled passengers' journeys had been affected by a lack of staff, but contingency plans had been put in place in all instances.[65] However, its figures are reliant on self-reporting by passengers, and do not take into account the extent to which passengers have been dissuaded from travelling by train completely. Anecdotal evidence of train companies' negligence of disabled passengers abound, such as the case of Jenny Skelton and Sammy Taylor, who arrived late at a disability pride event, having been left stranded at Seaford station by a driver-only-operated train.[66]

Conclusion

While there will always be conflict between workers and their employers, the strikes that caused Ruth, Sam and so many others such misery were entirely avoidable. The £256 million that the government was trying to save by cutting staff is a drop in the ocean compared with the huge increase in subsidy created by privatisation. When the cost to the taxpayer, the impact on the wider economy and the misery they caused passengers are taken together, the dispute was a massive waste of public and private resources, and all to make the railways less accessible at a time when sustainable transport should be opened up to a wider range of people.

There is also an important moral element at play here. While the focus of government policy has been on reducing staffing costs, this has not extended to the salaries of senior rail managers, which have escalated steeply since privatisation. For example, the highest-paid director at Northern received a salary of £248,000 in 2019, the year before the franchise was renationalised after widespread criticism of its mismanagement of services.[67] In 1979 the highest-paid staff member at BR, the chairman, earned £32,948 per annum,[68] or £170,475 in today's prices. That was the salary of the person responsible for the entire railway network and its operations, rather than just the infrastructure or one or two train operating companies. Reducing senior managers' salaries would make little difference to the overall financial position of the railways. But failure to do so gives credence to unions' portrayal of the unfairness of the treatment of rail workers.

To see railways as a social service for the benefit of all means putting railway staff, and the care and assistance they give to passengers, at the forefront of our thinking, not portraying them as an expensive inconvenience. Of course, rail unions such as the RMT should not be free of criticism. As an industrial union with some clout, the RMT is virtually alone in a country where the trade union movement has been ravaged by successive governments. This breeds a defensiveness and insularity in its culture, which can come across as uncaring and abrasive. In particular, although the RMT's focus on the technicalities of door operation during the guards' strike is understandable, it did little to foster solidarity among passengers and the general public. That support is crucial when it is up against the state and the vast resources it has at its disposal. It was up to groups of disability activists and fledgling passenger campaigns to flesh out the extent of the loss that driver-only operation would impose on the public.[69] As the strike progressed, the support from these groups seemed to change the way the RMT argued, increasingly emphasising the wider role of the guard and their importance to accessibility.[70]

The government, through its private operatives, went after guards because it needed to save money as a result of privatisation's vast wastage of public money, and because guards are an easier target than drivers. Nevertheless, simply renationalising railways does not prevent governments from attacking services and attacking staff, as can be seen in the history of BR or in publicly owned European systems today.[71] In a loss-making industry, there will always be pressure to reduce public subsidy and thereby to minimise the social service aspect of railways. If the past few years have taught us anything it is that better outcomes are achievable when rail workers do not take cuts lying down, and that rail workers are stronger when they fight alongside passengers in common cause.

4

How can the railways be held to account?

Without warning, our train jolts back to life. Ruth clasps the wood-effect table in front of her to reclaim her balance.

'We're moving', she exclaims, glowing with, perhaps, misplaced optimism.

'We've got to do something about it. Everyone likes a good moan on social media, but how many of us actually do something constructive to change things? In fact, no offence, but academics are the worst – you like to analyse what's wrong, but how can we make it right? I don't want to spend the rest of my life stuck on trains going nowhere.'

These are not easy questions to answer. But one thing's for sure: as this chapter will show, fundamental change will not come from within the industry or government. It's up to passengers like Ruth to become political animals and campaign with others.

Reform from above

It wasn't supposed to be this way: how 'the market' failed passengers

It's important to say first that the privatised railways were designed in a way that was supposed to make reform unnecessary. Markets are supposed to be 'self-correcting'. If companies start doing things in an inefficient manner by, for example, wasting raw materials or making things for which there is no demand, they will go out of business, leaving behind the most efficient and customer-responsive companies. Supporters of privatisation argue that, because they lack the discipline of the market, state-owned companies are inefficient and are unable to provide the things people need. In the case of rail privatisation, the main form of competition it created was between private companies bidding to run 'franchises' – services provided in particular geographic locations for a set period. Companies would bid for franchises on the basis of their own confidence that they could use their entrepreneurial flair to attract new customers, and find efficiency savings in their operations, better than other companies who bid. Any company that failed to deliver on its promises on service levels could be fined by the government agency responsible for franchising, and would be unlikely to win another contract.

This combination of franchise bidding competitions and regulation was supposed to make train operating companies provide the best service possible to passengers, forcing them to quickly correct any mistakes made. However, as this book has argued, the over-riding objective of franchising was not to improve services, but to save the government money. Indeed, this was written into the methodology used by the government to assess franchise bids. As a representative from a company bidding for the first franchises described,

[We thought that if we] could offer to improve the service in some way, presumably there might be some trade off in terms of the level of subsidy the government would be prepared to put in. I never saw any of that taking place. It was 'who will [accept] the lowest subsidy for taking this franchise off our hands?'[1]

There was an obvious risk in this approach: what if the company offering the largest subsidy reductions had been over-optimistic in its assumptions and was unable to deliver what it had promised? Indeed, that's what transpired. Companies won the right to run services by outcompeting their rivals in promising fantastic savings of public subsidy, only to admit after a couple of years that the contract had been financially unviable. Franchise agreements were structured so that most of the subsidy savings were contracted for their latter years. That meant that companies could skim off profits at the beginning of a contract, only to either walk away from the franchise – in which case the franchise was temporarily renationalised – or, as was more common, renegotiate the contract so that the promised subsidy reduction was taken out. Typically, the franchisee was able to renegotiate or walk away with meagre financial penalties. It was a case of 'heads they win, tails we lose'.[2]

Fines and contract termination can work only where they create significant financial pain for companies and their owners. But rail franchising was never able to do that, because the burden of financial responsibility it would have placed on companies would have been too high to attract enough bidders, and hence for franchise-bidding competitions to be considered 'competitive'. In the mad, circular logic of the privatised railways, fining companies is pointless, because it leads to fewer companies wishing to bid for franchises, which lowers the chances that governments can use the franchising system to save money.

Public outcry over private franchise collapses and public bailouts has pushed successive governments to tighten their grip on train operating companies. In an attempt to avoid over-optimistic bidding, train operating companies have been required to stump up cash at the beginning of franchise contracts so that it can be used as insurance against government bailout in the event of financial problems.[3] However, more onerous contractual conditions mean less prospect of profit, and that has meant fewer companies interested in bidding to run services. The result is that a dwindling number of international transport groups – including many that are publicly owned in other countries – are effectively taking it in turns to run Britain's passenger services, and with very little to offer in terms of service improvements.[4]

The franchising of passenger rail services promised that the entrepreneurial spirit of the private sector, harnessed through competition, would continually improve services. But it rested on a fatal logical flaw: that the private sector could improve upon the economic efficiency of BR to create better services and decrease subsidy at the same time. As successive governments found to their cost, the private sector would participate in the railways only if it could extract wealth from them with little financial risk, and any attempts to use bidding competitions to make it behave otherwise were doomed from the beginning. No transport system runs perfectly all of the time. Adjustments and reform are always necessary to correct mistakes and shift resources to meet changing demands, but this was never going to happen in the system of franchising that privatisation created.

Marking their own homework: industry-friendly inquiries

Popular anger about the state of the railways, as well as mounting costs and debt for the government, has led to several high-profile inquiries. These were supposed to learn lessons from past mistakes and recommend beneficial reforms. The problem for passengers is that the framing of the inquiries, and the personnel chosen to lead them, have focussed on making privatisation work, and so have foreclosed on the necessary condition of any meaningful improvement – public ownership.[5]

The first of these inquiries was launched in 2009. The New Labour government – still reeling from the railways' cost explosion following the Hatfield crash – announced a thorough review of options to make the railways more economically efficient. It appointed Sir Roy McNulty to head up the study.[6] McNulty is described in a critical review of his work as having 'earned his knighthood after passing several times through the revolving door between the civil service and the para-statal private sector'.[7] Unsurprisingly, given his background, McNulty did not propose major structural reform.[8] Indeed, as noted in Chapter 2, the main effect of his review was a government attack on rail staff.

The problem was not the level of detail of McNulty's study, or that there were not some useful ideas contained in it – it was the fact that he ruled renationalisation out of court. This was justified according to some strange reasoning. As he wrote: 'Given the cost reductions seen in other sectors from privatisation, it seems unlikely that renationalisation would lead to a reduction in costs … [It] is the extensive involvement of Government that has, to some extent, prevented the cost reductions seen elsewhere.'[9]

But this conflates different issues – whether or not private ownership is more efficient than public ownership, and whether government *interference* has made the *privatised* railway system less efficient.

On the first issue, McNulty claims that, in general, private companies are more efficient than state-owned companies. Only one source is cited in support – a regulatory report by the water regulator Ofwat, which itself provides no evidence to back up the claim.[10] Focussing on the railways, McNulty also claims that one study shows that 'where the government had been directly involved' in train operating company contracts – for example through re-negotiated franchise deals – 'there was deterioration in efficiency'.[11] However, the study actually states that the observed loss of efficiency may have resulted from 'a process of making good neglect of cleaning and maintenance of rolling stock and stations' which had occurred before the government took greater control of the franchises mentioned. In fact, the authors go on to comment that 'franchising does not seem to have succeeded in driving down train operating company costs'.[12] In his treatment of evidence here, McNulty displays what one group of commentators called his 'theological assumption' of privatisation's 'original virtue'.[13]

The second premise in McNulty's dismissal of public ownership is that government interference has prevented privatisation from reducing costs. There are some good reasons to be wary of overbearing central government interference in the railways. The most successful railway systems in the world are run on the basis of public ownership, with the management of the industry undertaken by public railway companies at arm's length from central government. Having a railway that is run from Whitehall offices, by civil servants with little industry-specific knowledge, is indeed potentially very problematic. It can lead to an abstract, accounting approach to management that struggles to understand the specifics of the sector and the people who work in it. But McNulty's pre-existing commitment to privatisation means that the study fails to get to grips with *why* central government came to take greater control over the railways as the privatised system developed.

Without very substantial and repeated government intervention, the rail system would have collapsed. Because of the surge in costs that privatisation produced, the government dispensed with most of the power of the supposedly independent Rail Regulator to set subsidy levels, and it had to guarantee Network Rail's ballooning private debts and take back control of failing franchises. In other words, the very high levels of government meddling in all aspects of the rail system were a result of the obsession with replacing public spending with private finance that has kept the privatisation show on the road for over two decades. BR had more autonomy from central government than the railways have today because it was publicly owned and publicly funded. The government set the overall subsidy, but it was BR itself that decided how to prioritise spending. To blame public ownership for government interference is an inversion of reality, albeit a useful one to those committed to pushing private finance into every corner of the rail system.

Indeed, McNulty envisaged little change in terms of Network Rail's financing arrangements. Remarkably, rather than highlighting the obvious unsustainability of its mounting debts, the study proposed pilot projects to bring in fresh forms of private finance, which it concluded might be made possible through fragmenting Network Rail into regional companies.[14]

McNulty's review set the tone for those that followed, for successive government-sponsored inquiries have flailed around looking for ways to patch up the privatised railway system in the face of deep and mounting crises.

In 2013 David Cameron's coalition government appointed Richard Brown, the former head of the rail franchising at the private transport company National Express and chair of the Rail Delivery Group.[15] Brown was tasked with bringing forward proposals to get franchising 'back on track as quickly as possible'.[16] Given this remit, it is not surprising that his recommendations included little fundamental change to the current system. Instead they implied tinkering around the edges, such as a suggestion for new franchise contract lengths.[17] The legacy can be seen today in continual franchise collapse and the lack of competition for contracts.

The next major review was Nicola Shaw's review of the finances of Network Rail after its forced renationalisation in 2014, covered in Chapter 1. As we saw, despite the fact that Network Rail's renationalisation and consequent funding crisis were created by its years of unsustainable private borrowing, Shaw's review did little to offer genuine solutions to the problem, except for vaguely speculating on the possibility of further private borrowing through new structures. The limitations of Shaw's work no doubt stemmed from the very constrained remit in which she was tasked to operate by David Cameron's austerity-obsessed government. However, it was also another example of elite industry figures marking each other's homework and keeping genuine solutions to the railways' crises off the table. Shaw was chief executive of the newly privatised High Speed 1 (HS1) railway line and had held leading positions at the Strategic Rail Authority and First Group.[18]

The latest major review was supposed to be a little different from the ones that preceded it. The Williams Review was launched in the aftermath of the 2018 timetable chaos, which the Tory transport secretary Chris Grayling admitted had 'severely damaged public confidence in the railways'.[19] The idea was to have a root-and-branch review of the structure of the railways and how they were governed and financed.[20] The chair was feted as a person of supreme business acumen and independence, being deputy chair of the well-regarded John Lewis group.[21] In truth, Keith Williams was little different from his predecessors, insomuch as he was very familiar with the public/private terrain of the 'regulated utilities' and privatised transport, having been chief executive officer and chairman of British Airways, and having been recently appointed to the board of Royal Mail.[22]

Tantalisingly, however, in this review, the prospect of renationalisation was 'on the table' among other options that Williams would consider.[23] The report faced a series of delays that were never explained. Rail policymaking and scrutiny of past problems were effectively on-hold until publication. As the Association of British Commuters, a passenger campaigning group, commented in 2020: 'The Williams Review was supposed to restore "trust" in the public and solve the structural chaos that caused the 2018 timetable collapse. However, the review was never published and as a result we are two years overdue some government accountability and a solution that urgently restructures the railway.'[24]

By the time it was finally published in 2021, the review bore little resemblance to the thorough inquiry promised three years earlier. It had been renamed the *Williams–Shapps Plan for Rail*, indicating that its conclusions were very much the joint work of the supposedly independent Williams and the new Tory transport secretary, Grant Shapps. Although it made some important recommendations (which will be discussed in Chapter 5), the grave errors of the past were left unscrutinised. Despite its promises, it turned out to be just the latest exercise in trying to get privatisation to work again. If passengers want serious reforms to fix Britain's railways, they will need to look beyond the tie-up between government, industry and private finance that has ruled rail policy for the past thirty years.

The compensation racket

As repeated government-sponsored inquiries have failed to deliver meaningful reform, and as the failure of the privatised rail system to work for its passengers has become ever more acute, the last few years have witnessed a rise in compensation culture.

A new compensation regime was introduced in the early days of privatisation, whereby passengers could receive a 20 per cent refund on their tickets if their trains were an hour or more late.[25] That was gradually improved on, with many operators now offering a 25 per cent refund on delays of fifteen minutes or more, and a full refund for delays of an hour or more.[26]

When asked by journalists about poor services, train operating companies are often keen to remind the public that compensation is available for delays.[27] Buying a rail ticket is a form of signing a contract: you pay a certain amount of money for the service of being transported from A to B. As with any contract, you have a right to seek redress if the service you were promised was not provided. Compensation can sugar the pill for passengers who have been inconvenienced. It also allows for just a little bit of revenge, kicking the rail companies where they hurt the most – their back pockets.

However, according to official figures, 63 per cent of passengers who are eligible for compensation don't claim it.[28] On our train, that means thousands of pounds' worth of compensation being left unclaimed. This is true for several reasons. First, many passengers are unaware that they have a right to compensation. Second, claiming a refund can be very complex. Consumer association Which? found that companies require passengers to provide up to twenty-four separate pieces of information to support a claim.[29] Third, the less passengers have paid for their tickets, the less they are likely to claim.[30] Why spend perhaps fifteen minutes filling out a compensation claim for a twenty-minute delay to your short local train journey, when the most you'll get back is 25 per cent of a £5 fare?

Recent reforms have made getting compensation a little easier, with many train operating companies automatically compensating passengers who hold advance tickets. This is possible because advance tickets are service-specific, so when a train is delayed the train operating company knows which passengers have travelled on it and how late it was. But things remain much more complicated for the vast majority of passengers who don't use service-specific tickets, who are required to actively apply for compensation themselves.

Around 60 per cent of delays are attributable to Network Rail, the infrastructure provider. When Network Rail causes delays, it compensates train operating companies to make up for their loss of earnings. While most passenger compensation isn't claimed, train operating companies receive 100 per cent of the compensation due to them.[31] This creates significant income for train operating companies, but they are not required to pass the resulting savings on to passengers through lower fares. This difference between the compensation received by train operating companies and the amount they pay as compensation to passengers has resulted in the companies pocketing around £1.1 billion in ten years.[32] Thanks to a lack of transparency in financial reporting, it is not known just how much of this was siphoned-off in profit. Importantly, it has also meant that there has been less financial incentive for train operating companies to work with Network Rail to reduce delays. What is the point of cooperation if you know you're going to be compensated for loss of income, and most of the money you get is for you, not your passengers?[33]

Which? has proposed a number of ways to ensure that passengers on non-advance tickets can receive automatic compensation for delays, including using 'technology' to track passengers' actual movements and asking season ticket holders to nominate their usual service.[34] But the questions these suggestions pose – do passengers want their movements tracked in this way? Isn't the whole point of a season ticket that you can catch any train? – only go to show that treating the continual difficulties passengers face as a consumer rights problem is farcical. People want a reliable and affordable train service, not to be financially compensated for not having one.

Perhaps the most insidious consequence of delay compensation is that it treats the railways' failings as having individual, rather than systemic and collective, impacts. We are encouraged to enforce our individual consumer rights and to think of the effects of bad rail service in purely monetary terms, when the impacts on our lives are much more fundamental – the strain it puts on personal relationships, the feeling of helplessness it generates – and are shared with others. A bad railway system is something that affects us all. Even those that don't use the rail system can benefit from the reduced road congestion that it causes. We have a shared interest in making it better, and that is arguably better served by collective effort than by individual complaints or compensation.

Reform from below

As this chapter has demonstrated, there are no channels within the railway system itself through which passengers can ensure that the railways are fixed. That means, as with many other groups in society whose needs are not being met, that rail passengers must engage with political campaigning if they want to ensure that things get better.

Formally speaking, passengers' interests are represented by Transport Focus, which styles itself as the 'independent watchdog for transport users'.[35] Although the organisation prides itself on its independence from government, which is true from a legal perspective, its board is directly appointed by the transport secretary.[36] Accordingly, it does not seek to take positions on the fundamentally political issues of government spending, who owns the railways and fare policy, all of which have been central to the analysis of passenger concerns in this book. Instead, it focusses on consumer research and consumer protection – a kind of *Which?* for transport – working to ensure that passengers know about the rights surrounding the use of their ever more expensive tickets. It does not seek fundamental change. That task is undertaken, to greater or lesser extents, by a ragtag collection of volunteer-led local and national campaigns.

Addressing the problems with our railways will require a step-change in political activism. For that, we need to understand what has worked so far and what hasn't, and what barriers to and opportunities for success exist. As the rest of this chapter will show, there are different approaches to rail campaigning, and in recent years, new types of movement have emerged which show that, for all the good work established campaigns have done, a more militant and daring style may now be required.

Old-school rail campaigning

If railway workers have been remarkably successful in defending working and conditions and pay since privatisation (as discussed in Chapter 3), rail campaigners have also been successful in preventing line closures and loss of services. Much of this campaigning started before privatisation when BR repeatedly threatened to close lines in response to ever greater pressure from central government to cut subsidy. Although the massive cuts to the railway network undertaken by Richard Beeching in the 1960s are rightly famous, BR pursued a policy of further cuts to supposedly uneconomic lines throughout the 1970s, albeit at a much slower pace.[37]

A major turning point in reversing this trend came as a result of a successful campaign to save the Settle–Carlisle line in the 1980s. This was a major intercity route from Yorkshire to Cumbria (for Glasgow and the west of Scotland) but had fallen on hard times. BR deliberately diverted services away from the route in order to make the case for a planned closure in 1984. But that was prevented by a big campaign by rail passengers. By 1989 the government had been forced to rescind the closure and make essential repairs to the line's dilapidated infrastructure.

Campaigners promoted and encouraged more passengers to use this very scenic line, which gives access to remote parts of the Yorkshire Dales National Park. Through this, they demonstrated latent demand, which encouraged BR to add more services, making closure more and more politically unviable. The net result of their efforts was that passenger numbers increased from 90,000 a year to over 1 million a year over the course of three decades.[38]

Since the campaigners' victory, very few railway lines or stations have closed across Britain. Not only has legislation made the closure process more arduous,[39] but, perhaps more importantly, railway line closures have become politically toxic.[40] In the language of political theory, the belief that railway lines should not close has become 'hegemonic'.[41] All major political parties are opposed to closure, because any other position would be electoral suicide.

With the threat of closures mostly off the table, rail campaigners have focussed on improving the existing network. A good example of successful local campaigning can be found in Lincolnshire, where the Friends of the Brigg & Lincoln Lines have won a restoration of weekday services to Gainsborough Central station. Gainsborough is a medium-sized town in Lincolnshire with a rapidly rising population.[42] Central station used to be a major stopping point for busy services between the East Midlands and the popular seaside resort of Cleethorpes. However, a mixture of cheap foreign package holidays and vicious cuts by BR rendered these services almost obsolete. From 1993, all that remained were three journeys each way on Saturdays only, operated by Northern in recent years. Although Gainsborough has another station – Lea Road – it is far from the town centre and has been badly neglected by operator East Midlands.[43]

The Friends' first victory was to improve the appearance and accessibility of Central station. The station once boasted substantial buildings, including covered platforms, and staff to sell tickets. But these were removed in 1975, and, by 1993 little remained of the former station, other than the tracks, the platforms and a dilapidated footbridge accessed only via steps. The only other passenger infrastructure consisted of two bus shelters with open sides. They kept passengers dry, provided the rain fell at exactly a ninety-degree angle to the platforms. The station even lacked basic signage. Having got nowhere by asking the railway powers that be to remedy the situation, the Friends took it upon themselves to make their own information signs, which was enough to embarrass Northern into installing some of its own.

The Friends' station improvement efforts combined with their attempts to promote the line to local people through a website and leaflets.[44] Together, these drove a 40 per cent increase in patronage between early 2013 and mid-2015.[45] Having been forced by the campaign to address the dreadful service at Gainsborough Central, Network Rail's managing director Alex Hynes told a local radio station that there were no plans for improvements because the company's focus was on commuter services elsewhere.[46] However, the Friends' campaigning eventually proved successful when, in 2019, weekday services to Gainsborough Central re-started, providing the first regular service to the town centre for twenty-six years. The hourly service would combine with services to Gainsborough Lea Road to provide a twice-hourly service to the town from Sheffield.[47]

The secret of the Friends' victory lay in the fact that those new services would not cost the government extra money in subsidy payments. It was discovered that trains that had hitherto terminated at nearby Retford, and would usually wait there for forty minutes, could be extended to Gainsborough Central and get back to Retford in the same time, and so no new rolling stock or extra staff would be required to run the new services.[48]

For the most part, 'Friends of' campaigns focus on modest efforts, such as helping to brighten up stations with paint and flowers – indeed there are hundreds of excellent examples of this across the network. But an inherent risk in local campaigning is that campaigners become simply unpaid railway workers, doing for free the things that railway companies are unwilling – or financially unable – to do, without ever really making the railways fundamentally improve. Indeed, the cost savings of voluntary labour were arguably part of the motivation for the rail industry when it created extensive 'community rail partnership' networks, which bring professional and voluntary work together. One study found that 3,200 volunteers provide 250,000 hours of labour on the railways every year, which would cost the railways £3.4 million a year if that work was paid for.[49]

The problem for campaigners is that any significant improvements in service quality and fares are bound to cost the government a lot of extra money and require it to end its deeply embedded obsession with privatisation and addiction to private finance. Many of the frustrations faced by campaigners are created at a higher, political level, and, in a fragmented, money-constrained industry, it is difficult to bring about positive change, even where the benefits are blindingly obvious.

Winning more, as opposed to just defending what we already have or providing voluntary labour, is so difficult because of the high financial and ideological price that rail campaigners' opponents would have to pay for losing. Recognising that fact means uncompromising campaigning that steers away from tinkering around the edges and seeks to establish a collective rail-user power to counter the powerful tie-up between government, industry and private finance that directs rail policy. In recent years, a number of movements have emerged which, however limited in scale, may point to the kinds of activities needed to turn things around.

The new breed

Early in the morning on Monday 22 January 2007, a bizarre sight greeted commuters at Bristol Temple Meads station, a hub of services for the First Great Western franchise. People had entered the station waving cardboard cut-out pictures of cows' heads. They were handing out what looked like train tickets, in the familiar tangerine-and white design. On closer inspection, these were fake tickets, printed with the destination to 'Hell and back' and issued by 'Worst Great Western' for travel in 'Cattle Class'. Passengers were being encouraged to use these free fake tickets rather than buy proper ones.

A combination of poor planning for timetable changes and bad availability of rolling stock meant that up to sixty trains a day were being cancelled in the Bristol area, causing extreme overcrowding. Compounding this misery, commuters had faced eye-watering fare rises of up to 12 per cent that year.[50] A group of passengers decided to do something about it and created a new campaign group called More Train Less Strain. The group quickly decided that the only way they would get First Great Western to listen would be to call a fare strike. Protestors gathered at stations in the Bristol and Bath area, using their fake tickets to persuade around 2,000 other passengers to join their strike.

Use of the fake tickets posed a dilemma for guards and ticket barrier operators. First Great Western warned passengers that travelling without a valid ticket risked prosecution, the maximum penalty being a £1,000 fine or a three-month prison sentence.[51] In practice, however, it appears that railway staff mostly turned a blind eye, presumably because they were sympathetic with the protesters' message.[52]

A year later, after little improvement to the service, the group repeated the stunt. Unable to stop the protests through enforcement, First Great Western instead attempted to belittle the strikers' efforts, claiming that 'less than 100 people refused to pay – out of 100,000 daily passengers'.[53] It was an odd statement, given that the company, just days before the second strike, made a number of important concessions. It apologised to passengers for service disruption and announced a doubling of season ticket compensation rates and an eleven-month fare freeze, all in an apparent attempt to appease passengers in order to reduce strike activity and its impact.[54]

The second strike was the last significant activity of More Train Less Strain, and the group petered out. Although a short-lived movement, it demonstrated that through militant refusal to pay fares, significant concessions could be wrested from train operating companies and, ultimately, the government.

In April 2014 South Yorkshire Passenger Transport Executive removed free travel on local trains for older and disabled people.[55] It was a disaster for thousands of people in the region, particularly those on low incomes. But an action group of retirees, many of whom were members of the 'trades council' (a local coordinating organisation for trade unions), started leafleting fellow passengers. After a lively meeting at Barnsley Library that attracted 300 people, the South Yorkshire Freedom Riders group was born.[56]

On the first day of the withdrawal of free travel, the group took sixty older and disabled people to Barnsley Interchange station with the intention that they would travel for free. They were met by police and a Northern Rail manager. The manager told the crowd that free travel would be allowed for that day. Buoyed by this initial win, the 'freedom rides' became a weekly event.[57] Like More Train Less Strain's actions, these fare strikes appear to have been given tacit support by railway staff. Indeed, Tosh McDonald, president of the train drivers' union ASLEF, even went along for a few rides himself.[58]

As the numbers grew on each weekly ride, Northern and the police opted for a hands-off, permissive approach. But on the fifth week, the Freedom Riders found a solid wall of police blocking the southbound platform, insisting that they pay to travel. Instead of doing so, the crowd crossed the footbridge and caught the next northbound train, giving the police a friendly wave as they left.

On 9 May 2014 the Transport Executive announced a U-turn, reinstating free travel for disabled passengers and half-fare travel for older passengers. It was a partial victory for the Freedom Riders, who then pushed for the restoration of fully free travel for older passengers as well.

After more successful freedom rides, the police took a tougher stance. On 23 June the Freedom Riders were 'kettled' by police, and two older activists were violently arrested and charged with 'obstruction and fare evasion'.[59] Such was the ferocity of the attack that some protestors required hospital treatment. A reporter from a local newspaper was ordered by a Northern representative to delete their video footage or face arrest under anti-terror laws.[60] A big campaign got the charges dropped just before the two activists were due to attend court.[61]

After these experiences, the Freedom Riders suspended their rides because the movement's participants were fearful of police violence. But rather than quietly going away, they built on the strength of their campaign and broadened its scope to protest against fare rises and cuts on local buses. In this way they quickly notched up further successes, winning free bus travel to hospitals before 09:30 with one bus company (concessionary bus travel usually starts after 09:30 on weekdays) and a flat £1 concessionary fare with many other operators. The Freedom Riders have also campaigned for public control of buses, alongside other groups.[62]

Branching out into campaigning on buses has been a feature of many recent rail-based campaigns. Buses outside London were deregulated in 1986, meaning that local authorities lost control over services, which were subsequently privatised. This led to huge service cuts and fare increases, with the result that bus use has since halved in urban areas. In contrast, in London, which was allowed to keep regulation, services remain relatively affordable and of high quality, and bus use accordingly doubled in the same period.[63] Such has been the disaster of bus deregulation that it has prompted an investigation by a former United Nations rapporteur on poverty. The report found that bus deregulation had 'left residents with an expensive, unreliable, fragmented, and dysfunctional bus system that is slowly falling apart'. As a result, (former) bus passengers have 'lost jobs, missed medical appointments, been forced out of education, sacrificed food and utilities, and been cut off from friends and family'.[64]

The Association of British Commuters was founded as a campaign group during the start of the collapse of rail services south of

London, in 2016. It has campaigned for political accountability and reform of the rail system in the interests of passengers, focussing in particular on lack of access for disabled people and de-staffing. Its tactics have included station protests, citizen journalism, which has revealed facts embarrassing to rail leaders, and supporting legal challenges to the rail industry. Like the South Yorkshire Freedom Riders, the group has also become involved in campaigning for public control of buses, alongside the We Own It anti-privatisation campaign. The 'Better Buses' campaigns have already won bus regulation in Greater Manchester, which will go towards creating a re-integration of public transport in the region.[65] We Own It is also linked to the wide-ranging and effective Get Glasgow Moving campaign for integrated, sustainable and socially focussed transport.[66]

What can we learn from these recent movements? If campaigners want to go beyond the limited and rather conservative terrain of traditional rail campaigning and start to win political demands which seriously challenge the short-term, cost-cutting, and private-finance-obsessed *status quo*, they should consider more militant tactics. Perhaps the most effective tactic is fare strikes. Although fare strikes lose train operating companies some revenue, their main impact is political – they attract huge media attention and gather widespread public support, much to the embarrassment of the railway establishment. The examples of More Train Less Strain and the South Yorkshire Freedom Riders attest to the effectiveness of fare strikes, as do other examples of their use around the world.[67] However, travelling without a ticket is a criminal offence, and perpetrators are liable to receive criminal records and in theory could even be imprisoned. That's where support from railway workers is vital – the National Conditions of Travel state that passengers do not need to hold a valid ticket if they are permitted to travel by 'an authorised member of staff'.[68] This gives some leeway to guards and ticket barrier staff to turn a blind eye or accept fake tickets, as seems to have happened in the cases mentioned above. Of course, showing such solidarity with fare strikers may pose disciplinary risks for rail staff. It is vital, therefore, that passenger-campaigners forge links of solidarity with staff by, for example, supporting railway workers' strikes where they occur.

The Freedom Riders story shows that the tactic of fare strikes must be employed carefully, following informed assessments of numbers participating and the potential for rail security and police to employ 'heavy handed' tactics. But it also shows that militant actions are more viable when passenger groups can make broad alliances with rooted community groups and trade unionists. This is important, because one of the difficulties of transport campaigning is that, although millions of people travel by train, very few would think of the word 'passenger' when asked to describe themselves. How we get around is but one aspect of our complex, often difficult, lives. And, unlike people at a workplace or a community centre, transport passengers confront each other daily as passing strangers, making collective organising difficult. Linking with community groups gives access to much more deep-rooted and stable networks of support.

In creating such coalitions, passenger campaigns are often drawn to making demands across a wider range of transport modes, especially buses. Why is that? Transport campaigners have long argued for the need for public transport to be integrated. All too often, however, rail and bus campaigns have been separate issues, perhaps partly as a result of the different ways they are governed. But it makes little sense, given that many rail users rely on buses to get them to and from the station. Moreover, despite the long-term decline in bus use that began with deregulation, for every trip made by train, 2.6 trips are made by local bus.[69] More people rely on the bus, which means bus campaigning has a wider, more locally rooted audience. Including buses in rail campaign work therefore creates the potential for deeper alliances with other groups such as trade unions and community campaigns committed to fighting social injustice.

Importantly, the new rail movements have shown that it is not necessary to wait for the right government to come in and sort the situation out. In the 2019 general election Jeremy Corbyn's Labour Party suffered a heavy defeat at the ballot box after a campaign which included pledges to renationalise mail, rail and energy firms. But the election was fought on a variety of fronts, especially on Brexit, and so can hardly be read as a rejection of all of Labour's policies. Indeed, opinions polls consistently show that the renationalisation of railways is a very popular policy, and even among Tory voters.[70] However, the point is that rail is a relatively niche political issue. Given the terrible social and environmental consequences of a broken rail system, campaigners do not have the luxury of hoping parliamentary politics will ride to the rescue.

Conclusion

Since privatisation, the rail industry has been run by a close partnership between central government and international finance. This ruling elite has proved incapable of the fundamental reform needed to significantly improve the industry. Governments have been too strongly wedded to financial fixes for the purposes of reducing subsidy in the short term, in which private finance has been an ever-willing partner. Giving passengers the platform for a collective voice in, let alone control over, rail policy would be too much of a threat to that cosy relationship. Unfortunately, passengers themselves have not been well enough organised to change that. Constrained by rail's marginal place in the transport system and by its geographical spread of its users, campaigners have traditionally tended to focus on modest station- or route-based reforms. While this has been an undoubted benefit to passengers, these voluntary efforts have always been in danger of being exploited by train operating companies, who are eager to boost ticket sales while cutting staff.

However, as the services have worsened and become ever more expensive to use, there have been examples of more militant campaigns emerging, whose partial successes provide inspiration. They have used tactics such as fare strikes, and have broadened their bases by embracing other transport demands, especially in relation to buses, and by linking to other social movements in communities. The challenge will be to generalise from these successes by building a national movement capable of winning a public transport system which is easy and cheap enough to use to provide a viable alternative to planes and cars.

Is there light at the end of the tunnel?

Having crawled along at a snail's pace for over an hour, we begin to pick up speed. Mercifully, we're nearly at our destination. Macclesfield's dim strip lights flashing by mean it's only half an hour to Manchester. The feeling on board is a mixture of relief and exhaustion. Passengers begin to stretch and yawn.

'Look, thank you for looking into this', Alisha tells me, shaking her arm to restore blood circulation. 'Good luck with the book. It's all a real problem, and people are fed up. But, from what you've said, there isn't much hope of things changing soon. There are too many special interests at play. But listen, good luck anyway.'

To be fair to Alisha, few people would be optimistic and energised after spending four hours cooped up with an academic banging on about their favourite subject. There are grounds for optimism, but what needs to change for Alisha and others to get the railway service they deserve?

The Great British fob-off

Recently, elite thinking has begun to accept some of the criticisms levied at the privatised railways. Given the state they are in and the massive public support for renationalisation, perhaps this should not be a surprise. This is best characterised by the publishing of the *Williams–Shapps Plan for Rail* in May 2021.[1] As discussed in Chapter 4, this is what had become of the Williams Review, which promised to bring accountability for the shocking degradation of services in many parts of the country in the mid- to late 2010s. But, instead of an independent inquiry, we have been presented with a government-sponsored 'plan', which is supposed to fix the troubled railway system.

The *Williams-Shapps Plan* is a thin document, but it contains some important changes to establishment thinking on the railways. It signals that the government intends to end franchising and reunite the management of passenger services with the infrastructure. By doing so, the plan could end some of the fragmentation and confusion that have plagued the railways since privatisation. A new public body called Great British Railways is set to take control of both passenger services and infrastructure, and will be run at arm's length from central government.

Yet this is not renationalisation. Great British Railways will run services through 'concessions', which private companies will bid for.[2] Supposedly, the key difference from the present franchising system is that Great British Railways will specify in detail the service to be provided, whereas under franchising train operating companies had more freedom to experiment with services. In fact, in recent years the government has come to specify services more and more, and so there won't be much difference in terms of who is in control of how services are provided. The main change is that Great British Railways will collect fares, with private companies being paid a management fee, regardless of how many passengers they carry. Given the dwindling interest of private companies in franchises in recent years, and how Covid-19 has hit train operating companies' finances, the plan can be seen as a move to re-enable private participation in the railways. It will re-privatise the many franchises that have ended up under state ownership thanks to the failure of franchising. This is no BR version 2.0.

The most troublesome implications of the *Williams-Shapps Plan* are in what it does not say. Most importantly, there is no plan for what to do about the dire state of railway finances. The report insists that £1.5 billion a year could be saved through the simplified structure it proposes, although the calculations behind this figure have not been published.[3] But that sum is minuscule in the context of the railways' financial crisis. As discussed in Chapter 1, by the time of the Covid-19 outbreak, public subsidy paid to the railways was totalling £13 billion per year, around four times more than had been required by BR. The last thing the railways needed was the sudden loss of income caused by the social distancing and work-from-home requirements that dealing with the pandemic entailed. The railways' lack of income pushed subsidy still higher, to £22 billion in financial year 2020/21.[4] By the time the *Williams-Shapps Plan* was published, train operating companies had been operating on temporary skeleton timetables, partly in recognition of reduced demand and partly due because of increased staff sickness. In December 2021 the government took advantage of the lack of demand and ordered train operating companies to permanently reduce services and make significant cuts in staffing levels.[5] In sharp contrast to the plight of rail staff, who have been pressured to take voluntary redundancy, and the passengers losing services, stands the fate of private train operators and rolling stock companies, which have been almost entirely shielded from the collapse of the industry by government bailouts.

Taken together, the *Williams–Shapps Plan* and subsequent government actions present a confused mix of nationalistic boosterism, unflinching support for private rail companies and their investors and drastic cuts to meet Treasury diktat.

The underlying cause of all of these actions is a failure in elite thinking to answer the question *what should the railways be for in early to mid-twenty-first-century Britain*? It is only through providing an answer that we can properly answer the questions the *Williams–Shapps Plan* was incapable of addressing: how much money is needed for the railways? Who should pay? And how should they be managed?

What are railways for?

Railways have come a long way since their debut as a serious form of passenger and freight transport nearly 200 years ago. In that time, they have served various functions, from being the motive force of the industrial revolution to supplying war efforts and, later, taking a secondary role to provide government-subsidised transport alongside the development of mass motorisation.[6] There is no reason to believe that the role of the railways will not change again, but what might that new role be? This is a matter for debate, but surely any comprehensive plan for the railways must be based on how they can support wider policy objectives?

This final chapter argues that the crisis that the railways face occurs at a particular historical juncture, which is characterised by two overarching major crises. The first is the climate emergency, which threatens to quickly undermine the prospects of our species' very survival, and the second is a wealth inequality and cost-of-living crisis, in which millions of British citizens are being pushed into severe material insecurity.

Before discussing what the railways need to do, we should first dwell on the challenges each of these crises throws up.

The climate emergency

The scale and urgency of the climate emergency are truly har-rowing. There cannot be a more important problem to overcome through public policy. Every part of the economy will need to change to avert its worst effects. Thanks to the burning of fossil fuels by humanity, the planet is already 1.1 degrees Celsius warmer than before industrialisation. That might not sound like a lot, but it represents a huge increase in energy which is already destabilis-ing our climate, making extreme weather events more likely. In the 2015 Paris Agreement, the world's governments committed them-selves to limiting this warming to 2 degrees Celsius, and ideally to no more than 1.5 degrees. The 2021 Intergovernmental Panel on Climate Change report spells out the consequences of not taking immediate action to reduce greenhouse gas emissions – mostly carbon dioxide. Unless we take serious action to drastically cut carbon emissions, we will continue to move head first into a world of extreme weather events, crop failures and food shortages, and economic insecurity. Every one-tenth of a degree Celsius takes us closer to a situation of runaway climate change, where the instiga-tion of climate feedback loops would ensure that there would be nothing we could do to prevent the total collapse of earth's life-support systems.[7]

The UK government is committed to meet 'net zero' by 2050, which would involve a 78 per cent reduction in greenhouse gases from 1990 levels by 2035. However, policies currently in place will cut only a fifth of the required emissions. Moreover, Britain has very high 'historical emissions' and so needs to go faster in reducing emissions than many other countries. Therefore something much closer to a 'net zero' 2030 target is more appropriate.[8]

Official figures, as represented in Figure 5.1, show that, following a phasing-out of coal-fired power stations, transport is now the economic sector with the highest emissions of greenhouse gases, and competes with agriculture for the sector that has been the least successful in decarbonising its activities in the last thirty years.[9] Note that the dip in transport emissions which took place in 2020 can be explained by the effect of lockdowns on transport demand, rather than lower greenhouse gas emissions per journey. We should expect to see emissions from transport rebound significantly (albeit not entirely, given the reduction in commuting created by increased working from home).[10]

Before moving on to think about what rail needs to do, we need a basic understanding of how the transport system as a whole will need to change to achieve rapid decarbonisation. A reduction in higher-emitting forms of transport will necessitate an increase the provision of other lower-emitting forms. In the language of transport policy

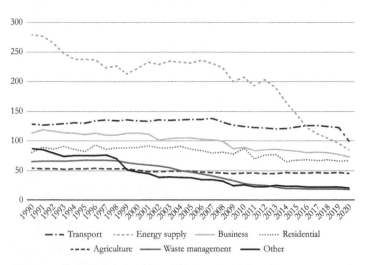

Figure 5.1 Estimated territorial greenhouse gas emissions by source category, by million tonnes carbon dioxide equivalent, UK, 1990–2020.

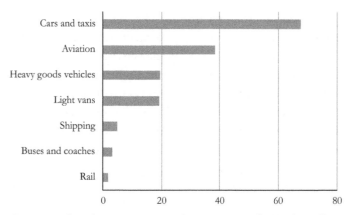

Figure 5.2 Greenhouse gas emissions by transport mode, UK, by million tonnes carbon dioxide equivalent.

this is known as 'modal shift', and planning for it means not treating each transport mode as a separate policy silo. Figure 5.2 breaks emissions down by transport mode. As can be seen, the biggest emitters are passenger motor vehicles, aviation and road freight.[11]

There is an unfortunate tendency in public discourse to assume that technological improvements will mean that we can more or less keep travelling and moving things in the same way, while simultaneously reducing our carbon emissions to safe levels. But that is a fantasy.

In terms of cars, electric vehicles are touted as the major solution. To be sure, electric vehicles have an important role to play in a future transport system, especially for the kinds of journeys even a vastly improved public transport network would find difficult to provide – for example very rural journeys and ambulance transport. But the way electric vehicles are talked about by politicians and the car industry often suggests that they could simply replace motorcars with electric vehicles on a 'like for like' basis. However, there aren't enough global mineral resources for all of the batteries that would be needed for a 'like for like' replacement of everyone's car, and the energy required would put huge pressure on the electricity network, which itself has to fully decarbonise and provide energy for other, more energy-efficient forms of transport (including rail).[12]

The limitations of the electric vehicle revolution also pose problems for decarbonising road freight. Batteries are incapable of providing the power needed by the vast number of heavy goods vehicles on our roads. Similarly, the privatisation of the postal sector has opened the way for widespread use of demand-responsive logistics companies like Amazon. While that is convenient for us as consumers, it has also added huge numbers of extra vehicles to the roads, which face the same limitations on battery and electricity availability as cars.

Aviation is also a massive problem in the context of the climate emergency. While the UK's total emissions have decreased by 39 per cent since 1990, and those of its domestic transport by 3 per cent, emissions from UK international aviation have increased by 138 per cent over the same period.[13] Promises of 'jet zero' – decarbonised flying – are a fallacy.[14] While it's conceivable that there may be some future technology that allows zero-carbon flying, it's not going to be available in the next decade or so, when we will need to make nearly all of the cuts to transport emissions required.

Social inequality

Before the Covid-19 outbreak there were 14.5 million people living in poverty in the UK.[15] At the time of writing, the temporary system of government assistance paid to people while Covid-19 ravaged the economy is being withdrawn just as a cost-of-living crisis hits, represented by rampant increases in the price of energy, housing and food, driving millions more to foodbanks, including, increasingly, those in paid employment.

An important part of this picture of economic precariousness is increasing 'transport poverty', caused by rising public transport fares and cuts to public transport services. Transport poverty occurs where people can't access transport, because either public transport does not exist or it is too expensive to use, and people cannot afford or are unable to use private transport, such as cars, and this prevents them from accessing essential activities like work, education, healthcare, shopping and services.[16]

Research by academics for the Joseph Rowntree Foundation has shown that people from more disadvantaged groups make considerably fewer trips than those from more affluent social groups. This was not found to be caused by reduced travel requirements, but rather by factors preventing trips from being made, such as lack of access to public transport.[17] Different socio-economic groups have differing levels of access to transport options, with those on lower incomes less likely to be able to afford a car and thus completely reliant on public transport, walking or cycling.[18] Households with no car make 30 per cent fewer trips and travel 60 per cent less in terms of distance than households with a car.[19]

Even in households that have access to a car, this is often not enough to cover all the journey requirements of all the family members. Although gender differences in car driving are declining, women are still less likely than men to be the main driver in a household,[20] meaning that they are more reliant on lifts from men in the absence of alternative transport options. Older and younger people face similar exclusions.

As the public transport system has become more expensive to use and less available, car ownership among the poorest in society has grown. In 2011 31 per cent of the poorest 10 per cent of households owned a car, and the proportion increased to 35 per cent by 2018.[21] This is a reflection of what has been labelled 'forced car ownership', where people buy a car out of necessity rather than choice.[22] A study of deprived areas in Glasgow found that residents were forced into car ownership because the public transport system was unable to support complex lifestyles, especially for households with children.[23] Another study reports that households on lower incomes that have access to frequent bus services are much less likely to own a car than households with similar income levels that do not.[24] The effect of forced car ownership it to push financially struggling households further into poverty. For households that have a car, the car is their second highest area of expenditure after housing.[25] In fact, the notion of 'car ownership' is a misnomer, because most drivers in fact lease their vehicles through finance. This pushes car drivers on lower incomes into higher levels of debt and consequent financial insecurity.[26]

A car-dominated society also leads to 'community severance'. Community severance has been defined as 'the separation of residents from facilities and services they use within their community' by a car-dominated environment, characterised by dangerous roads that are difficult to traverse on foot or by bike.[27] Community severance leads to social isolation,[28] with detrimental impacts on mental health. Car-dominated societies also create poor physical health outcomes. High car use contributes to the growing obesity crisis because, unlike public transport, it encourages door-to-door journeys without the physical exercise of walking and cycling. Urban areas are also blighted by the dangerous levels of air pollution produced by motor vehicles, which disproportionately affects poorer households.[29]

In short, the increasing dominance of motor vehicles over all aspects of our lives has compounded growing social and economic inequalities, while a lack of reliable alternatives is increasing social isolation, leaving significant sections of the population without the ability to access jobs and services.

The need for a 'just transition'

Many of the things that need to be done in order to both avert the worst impacts of the climate emergency and reduce inequalities are the same. For example, reducing carbon emissions would necessitate the mass retrofitting of the housing stock so that it is properly insulated. This would not only reduce our reliance on carbon-based energy, but also lift millions of people from fuel poverty. But both problems can be tackled properly only if they are thought about and acted upon at the same time, which would necessitate public, government-funded programmes. The alternative – of making households pay for their own retrofitting – would not only push poorer families into more poverty and debt, but also probably fail on decarbonisation, since it is the poorest households which inhabit the least energy-efficient housing.[30]

Sharing the costs and benefits of climate action has been called a 'just transition'. It is a growing demand of social movements worldwide, and one that has become increasingly mainstream.[31] In transport, achieving a just transition would be tricky. For example, simply increasing the costs of driving without improving public transport risks further impoverishing those on already low incomes who are forced to use a car – something that led to the *gilets jaunes* protests in France, for example. Rapid decarbonisation also means a loss of jobs in sectors that cannot continue to operate at the same scale, such as the aviation and car manufacturing industries. Ensuring that an equal or higher number of jobs is available in public transport to those workers would be key to ensuring that decarbonisation decreases social inequalities, rather than make them worse.[32]

It is in identifying its role in a just transition that the railways should focus if they are to remain relevant to society's needs. The next section will suggest how this could be achieved.

A just transition in transport

What would a new railway system that meets the challenges of a just transition look like? We need to start from an understanding that, although they have been treated as such, railways are not an isolated policy area. Firstly, they are part of a wider public transport system, relying heavily on bus and metro connections to help people travel from door to door. Panning out further, public transport is part of the overall transport system. Most fundamentally, transport is the thing that allows society and the economy to move and function. Any big changes to the transport system affect how people are able to function in society, and how the economy works.

This considered, a plan to revitalise the railways for the purpose of achieving a just transition has to be made in conjunction with similar efforts in other areas of the economy. We have a carbon budget with a hard limit, and any decision made that slows decarbonisation in one sector means that another sector has to work harder to decarbonise. These trade-offs have to be coordinated – the climate doesn't care where these emissions cuts come from, but we do, not least because decarbonisation creates a multitude of short-term winners and losers.

The big problem for transport decarbonisation is that for the past 100 years, the geography of Britain has been changed to make access to housing, jobs, retail and services as convenient as possible by car. This has created 'urban sprawl', where walking and cycling trips between amenities become very long, and lack of density and mass car ownership make public transport inefficient.[33] Therefore, if transport is to decarbonise, it is not only transport that needs to change but also the things that transport serves. For example, how land is allocated through the planning system needs radical reform, as does how public authorities choose to site public services.

Recognising this need for cross-sector coordination to tackle the climate emergency, the Campaign Against Climate Change has called for a National Climate Service. The idea is inspired by National Health Service. The National Health Service was created in the depths of austerity after the World War II as a publicly owned, free-to-use service which nationalised and coordinated a plethora of hitherto dysfunctional and disparate private health services, in line with other forms of social policy that together formed the 'welfare state'. As the campaign argues, despite the considerable funding challenges that the National Health Service faces, 'it is difficult to imagine how society would have responded to a health crisis such as the Covid-19 pandemic without a nationally coordinated, publicly-funded health service'. Of course, the climate emergency presents an even greater crisis. But so far, the response to it has been 'reliant on the free market and government departments, which consistently fail to prioritise the crisis or to plan any coherent, serious response to it'.[34] A National Climate Service would overcome both failings by being both a public sector provider of services (for example through a national programme to insulate all homes) and a coordinator of the national effort to decarbonise the economy in national and local government and the private and charitable sectors. As such, it would coordinate the activities of the Department for Transport in Westminster, and its equivalents in the devolved nations, with the activities of local transport authorities across the UK, in lock-step with its work in other sectors.

Because of the importance of both coordinating with, and balancing the remaining carbon budget between, other sectors of the economy, it is inappropriate to be too prescriptive when deciding how the railways, and transport more generally, should respond to the climate emergency to achieve a just transition. However, there are some measures which are probably unavoidable. These are to reduce overall travel demand, to take action to severely reduce car driving and flying, to join up public transport and to make public transport much cheaper and easier to use. Let us take these in turn before moving on to what the railways can do specifically.

Reduce travel demand

Before we think about what kind of transport system we need – and rail's place in it – it is worth asking whether we need to travel as much as we do. In the decade preceding the onset of Covid-19, each person in England travelled on average 6,600 miles per year, with little variation from year to year. But this plummeted to 4,334 miles in 2020. The reduction was driven by a 160 per cent decrease in commuting miles and a 147 per cent decrease in leisure travel miles.[35] Of course, much of this was due to lockdowns, which, at times, forced us to remain indoors and, at others, discouraged us from working in offices and pursuing indoor leisure activities. There is now plenty of evidence that the experience of working from home was positive for many employers and employees, meaning that commuting is unlikely to ever return to the levels seen before the Covid-19 pandemic. More than 80 per cent of employers have adopted 'hybrid working' recently – most during the pandemic – and intend to keep it, regardless of the progress of the virus.[36] And this has translated into changed commuting patterns as measured by transport mode. By early 2022, with most Covid restrictions lifted, workday travel was at just 47 per cent of pre-pandemic levels for rail and tube, and at 81 per cent for cars.[37]

Working from home has significant potential to help reduce transport-related carbon emissions. For example, one study estimates that the new patterns of home working could lead to a permanent 14 per cent reduction in morning commuter car trips – reducing traffic to school half-term levels.[38] A National Climate Service approach would recognise the decarbonisation benefits of working from home, while trying to maximise this positive development with coordinated supportive measures. One example would be the development of improved and cheaper broadband, with discounts for people using it for work. Another would recognise the limitations of working from home (such as lack of space and the costs of heating) by creating free-to-use community workspace hubs.

Workspace hubs are an example of a feature of what some have called 'fifteen-minute neighbourhoods'. A fifteen-minute neighbourhood policy aims to reverse the transport problems created by urban sprawl by ensuring that the most commonly used services, such as shops, post offices and social services, are located within a fifteen-minute walk of residents' homes.[39] Fifteen-minute neighbourhoods would considerably reduce the need for everyday driving, but would need significant coordination efforts to bring about, for which something like a National Climate Service would be essential. Localisation would also be a key component of decarbonising freight, with goods produced much closer to where they are consumed.

Take action to severely reduce car driving and ban short-haul flights

A reduction in demand for travel through working from home and fifteen-minute neighbourhoods would also need to be accompanied by serious action to meet the remaining demand (which would be considerable) by shifting car and plane journeys to sustainable forms of transport.

The government is currently facing a tough problem when it comes to Vehicle Excise Duty (what is commonly, though incorrectly, referred to as 'road tax'). Vehicle Excise Duty is a tax on vehicle emissions. That means electric car drivers don't pay it, and since the government's policy is to ban the sale of all diesel and petrol cars, it stands to lose £30 billion a year of Excise Duty revenues.[40] This has prompted serious discussions in central government over the practicalities of pay-per-use road pricing.[41] However, the way the government is looking at it – as essentially a form of revenue generation – will not be sufficient for a just transition. Although it could act as an incentive to cut driving, the revenues it generates could also act as an incentive for government to continue to promote driving and build roads. Road pricing will work for a just transition only if government accepts that it will lead to a loss of government revenue from motorists. In terms of road policy, much more can be done to encourage people out of cars and into sustainable forms of transport, for example by reallocating road space for bus and bike lanes.[42]

Aviation is another area where increasing taxes may not be a magic bullet for decarbonisation. Campaigners have long called for a 'frequent flier tax' or an 'air miles levy'. Both seek to target the amount of flying that individuals undertake. This matters because only 1 per cent of the world's population causes 50 per cent of commercial aviation emissions.[43] Those with greater incomes tend to fly more often and over longer distances, and so higher taxes on flights targeting those who cause the most environmental damage could be effective. However, this would take a lot of international agreement. Something that could be implemented immediately is a ban on short-haul flights.[44] For example, it's crazy that – despite the fact that the journey times from city centre to city centre are roughly the same, two thirds of people prefer to fly between London and Edinburgh rather than catch the train.[45] But given the urgency of the climate emergency and the disproportionate contribution of aviation to it, we should also ban flights where rail is less time-competitive but nevertheless can provide a reasonable service, meaning a ban on domestic air travel as well as a ban on air travel to our closer European neighbours.[46]

Joined-up public transport, with free electrified bus travel

Public transport needs to be integrated if it is to offer a useful service, but all attempts to integrate a privatised public transport system over many years have manifestly failed. In the face of the climate emergency we cannot afford more messing around. With a unified national public transport operator, coordinated by the National Climate Service, seamless journeys could be provided, with buses and trams connecting at railway stations and running in coordination with train schedules. You should not, for example, be penalised for missing your booked train because your bus was late, or be expected to wait a long time when changing. Public owner-ship of public transport is a prerequisite for creating user-friendly transport interchanges, with seamless rail, bus and tram transfers, free-to-use hire bikes and access to electric taxis for harder-to-reach places. This is not to suggest something revolutionary – for decades, other European countries have been providing efficient, integrated systems, although creeping privatisation has begun to threaten the cohesiveness of their systems too.

Reacting appropriately to the climate emergency through a just transition means looking for transport solutions that cut the largest quantity of carbon emissions at the fastest rate and with the greatest social benefits. Although radical rail reform is a necessary condition for a just transition, it is the radical reform of buses which would make the greatest strides to achieving a just transition in transport. More people use the bus than the train, and buses have the flex-ibility to quickly create new routes to meet rapidly changing social needs and transport policy priorities. It is also possible to create bus infrastructure very quickly by re-allocating road space from cars. Although it is likely that many bus routes will need to be operated by battery-powered vehicles, the most energy-efficient way to power electric buses is through fixed cables – in other words, as 'trolleybuses', and installing that infrastructure should be a priority. Recent experiments in road freight suggest that heavy goods vehicles can be powered in the same way, potentially alleviating some of the capacity stresses on the rail network that full decarbonisation implies.[47] New cycling infrastructure could also enable carbon-free 'last mile' light deliveries, as is already common in many European cities.

To rapidly reverse the downward spiral of bus use would mean incentivising use through free local bus travel. The idea that local buses can be provided for free is gaining in popularity. Indeed, by 2017 nearly 100 fare-free local public transport systems had been implemented worldwide, some on a trial basis and some permanently. Almost all of these experiments have resulted in increased use – with some impressive results in terms of getting people out of cars – and the economic costs are not as onerous as might be assumed.[48] But free local buses are a non-starter if they mean the continued involvement of private companies in running services. As with private rail companies, costs are increased not only by private bus companies' need to reward shareholders, but also by the significant costs of bidding and contracting that go alongside all types of public–private provision.

A rail system fit for a just transition

Now that we have sketched out what the overall transport system would look like according to a just transition, it is finally time to understand what part the railways could play.

Electrification

Railways are an extremely energy-efficient means of carrying large quantities of people and goods on medium to long distances, especially when they are electrified. With electricity provided by renewable resources, electrified rail transport is zero-carbon. However, thanks to decades of under-investment and privatisation, the British rail network is under-electrified. Only 38 per cent of routes are powered by electricity, while the rest rely on carbon-intensive and polluting diesel power. The average for other European networks is 55 per cent.[49] For many years, the government has had a formal policy to increase electrification. In reality, major electrification projects have been cancelled, scaled back and 'postponed'. This is due to a combination of a lack of funding and the stop-start nature of the roll-out, which has unnecessarily increased costs.[50] Figure 5.3 shows the amount of electrification that has taken place on the British rail network over the decade from 2010/11 to 2020/21.

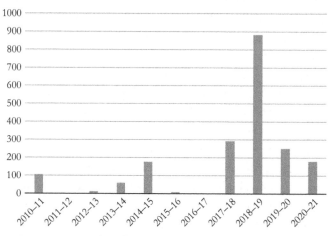

Figure 5.3 New electrification track kilometres, 2010/11–2020/21.

Apart from an impressive result in 2018/19, when a number of projects were completed at the same time, the record has been woeful, averaging 197 kilometres a year. At that rate, it will take another thirty-five years to complete the 13,000 kilometres of electrified lines recommended by Network Rail – which is far too slow to deal with the climate emergency.[51] If much faster electrification of the network seems far-fetched, consider that India's state-owned railways have electrified 46,000 route kilometres in the eight years between 2014 and 2022 – nearly three times the length of the entire British network – and have a target of an additional 6,000 kilometres every year.[52]

Expansion

With the rail system's source of power figured out, what kinds of services will the railways need to operate? Here it is tempting to join in with a chorus of calls to 'reverse Beeching' and for a massive expansion of new lines.[53] However, when it comes to rail infrastructure, the climate emergency unfortunately makes things more complicated than that. Building new railways is extremely energy-intensive and includes very high 'embodied emissions', especially from building materials like concrete and steel.[54]

To give an example, the government forecasts that the carbon emissions of High Speed 2 (HS2) will exceed its carbon savings over its 120-year projected lifetime. This increase in carbon emissions would need to be found by more extensive cuts in other parts of the economy.[55] That's partly to do with the energy requirements of the immediate construction process, but also with the energy required to provide the building materials that construction uses, especially concrete. Concrete is a hugely carbon-intensive construction material, currently responsible for 8 per cent of the world's carbon dioxide emissions. HS2 is trialling forms of lower-carbon 'green concrete', but – like zero-carbon aviation fuel – this has never been proved at scale.[56] It's possible that future technology could help us decarbonise construction. But that doesn't help us now.

This is not to argue that no new rail infrastructure is needed, but simply to question whether new infrastructure is currently being commissioned in the right way. It's also not an argument that the HS2 project should simply be abandoned. Opponents of HS2 argue that the significant 'sunk costs' that have already gone into the budget should not stand in the way of abandoning a scheme which, according to a recent estimate, could end up costing an incredible £106 billion.[57] However, just as important are the sunk carbon costs – once some of our carbon budget has already been spent, we then need to use that infrastructure as efficiently as possible to cut carbon emissions. There is a carbon-accounting argument that since the sunk carbon costs are significant, and HS2 will add capacity to the network, then it is sensible to complete the project, or at least the partially constructed first leg from London to Birmingham.

Given the time and carbon budget restrictions, much of the building work on the railways other than HS2 would probably involve expansion of existing routes by, for example, adding more tracks and relieving capacity bottlenecks at junctions by improving trackwork. All of these measures could significantly increase capacity while using relatively low amounts of embodied carbon,[58] as would electrification (because electric trains accelerate faster than diesel trails, freeing up extra track capacity). But there may be instances where it is sensible to open new lines for passenger traffic. New lines would need to target the kinds of journey where rail is most energy-efficient and socially useful – in moving large amounts of people frequently. These would generally be either new suburban or intercity routes, not rural routes to areas where relatively few people live. Given the speed of construction required, and the low proportion of our carbon budget available to undertake that construction, we would probably also be looking at reopening lines, rather than building entirely new ones. The following suggestions of currently non-funded schemes are not meant to be exhaustive, but to provide a flavour of the kinds of scheme needed to help create a just transition:[59]

- Matlock to Buxton. This would involve replacing 13 miles of missing track of the Midland Railway line, providing much better connections between population centres in the East Midlands and north-west.[60]
- Leicester to Burton-on-Trent. Reopening this mothballed line would link large settlements in the East Midlands, including some of the largest in Britain without a railway station.[61]
- The Woodhead route. Reopening this major railway line between Manchester and Sheffield would significantly improve transport capacity between Greater Manchester and South Yorkshire, and is a much more sensible idea than the mooted Transpennine road tunnel.[62]
- Okehampton to Bere Alston. This would provide an alternative route to Plymouth and the south-west avoiding the Dawlish line. Climate change means rising sea levels and more extreme storms, and already the Dawlish line is frequently closed for repairs, but it is probably unviable in the long term.[63]
- Edinburgh Suburban Railway. This line runs in a loop through Edinburgh's southern suburbs. A restoration of passenger services could form a useful part of the urban transport network.[64]
- Walsall to Water Orton. Reopening this derelict line would connect significant population centres in the West Midlands.[65]

- Skelmersdale spur. Skelmersdale was built as a new town based on cars, and so it has no closed railway formation running near the town centre. However, a short new line to the existing network would provide rail travel to its 40,000 inhabitants.[66]

Fares

A very quick and easy way to boost rail capacity, and make a greater contribution to a just transition, would be to abolish first class. First-class travel is an anachronism from the early days of the railways, when rail travel was a form of luxury consumption. In recent decades, first class has been a useful money generator, allowing the railways to profit from wealthy business travellers. But situations where standard-class carriages are full to bursting, while first-class carriages remain virtually empty, were already infuriating passengers before the Covid-19 pandemic hit.[67] In view of the urgent need to shift car and plane journeys to rail, first-class travel's enormous waste of energy and capacity must surely come to an end. A start could be made by immediately de-classifying all services, while a programme of refurbishments to convert first-class carriages to the higher-capacity standards of standard class could begin in earnest. The abolition of first class would also provide opportunities to create space for parcels, more bike storage and children's play facilities.[68]

More than anything, a just transition on the railways needs a major transformation of fares. According to Network Rail, by February 2022 leisure rail travel had returned to 90 per cent of its pre-pandemic levels. However, commuter revenue has remained severely depressed, with takings plateauing at around 50 per cent of pre-pandemic levels.[69] Given that these figures relate to a time when most lockdown restrictions have been lifted, they are likely to reflect a 'new normal' of home working and less peak-time commuting.

This is a massive problem for the railways, because around half of all fare income is from the types of ticket most closely associated with weekday commuting – anytime and season tickets.[70]

Lack of passenger demand as a result of Covid-19 lockdowns meant that the government had to increase subsidy by around £10 billion, almost doubling the railways' income from taxpayers, which was already around four times higher than before privatisation.[71] Although the return of off-peak travel and partial resurgence of peak travel are set to reduce this subsidy requirement somewhat, a higher subsidy than was needed before to Covid-19 is here to stay.

Any realistic, sober assessment of the collapse of peak travel would recognise that treating commuters as a cash cow is no longer viable. Rather than having trains cart around empty seats, the government could have abolished peak fares to encourage a shift from car use to public transport for those who still have to travel at rush hour. Instead, it has attempted to bribe former commuters back with free bacon sandwiches and mindfulness apps, while simultaneously increasing fares.[72]

But a just transition approach to reforming the railways would probably need to go further still on fares. In view of the untold and irretrievable costs that will be imposed on current and future generations if we do not rapidly reduce car use, a sensible a place to start would be to *set rail fares at half the estimated cost of driving a car for the same journey.* Given the need to both rapidly decarbonise and take the social consequences of transport policy seriously, car travel, as a heavily polluting and inefficient form of transport, should be much more expensive to use than (potentially) zero-carbon rail travel. To take our journey as an example, the cost of driving from Manchester to London and back would have been £55.70 per person, at 2022 prices. This is calculated by taking the mileage and multiplying it by the average price of fuel for the average car, adding average annual fixed costs such as purchase and depreciation, tax and MOT, calculated on a per-mile basis (by dividing average fixed costs by average mileage, and multiplying by the distance travelled), and assuming average car occupancy rates.[73] So, under the new regulation, a return journey to London from Manchester should not cost more than £27.85 – much less than the current off-peak (£94.50 at the time of writing) and peak (£374.40) returns. A return from Stockport to Manchester should not cost more than £0.94 – only 14 per cent the current off-peak day return (£6.90) and 10 per cent of the peak day return (£9.50). Free travel for older and disabled people, and children, should also be considered.

If it seems to some that these prices are unrealistically low – that they will take us from fares that are far too expensive to fares that are 'too cheap' – that's because we are socially conditioned to expect low-cost driving. Low-cost driving is a result of a political consensus which completely ignores the devasting socio-economic consequences of mass motoring and uses huge quantities of public and private resources to prop up the car manufacturing industry and provide car infrastructure, the vast majority of which is paid for through general taxation. And, while train travel has some advantages over car travel, such as allowing passengers to move without having to concentrate on the road ahead, and beating traffic at rush hour, generally speaking, driving is much the more convenient option for most trips and should be priced accordingly in relation to train travel. The beauty of setting rail fares at half the cost of car travel is that it shows the very real relationship between the two in terms of environmental impact, making much more explicit the choices we face when deciding how to direct society's resources for providing transport.

Of course, there is a 'revenue-neutral' approach to this, which keeps rail fares the same while massively increasing the cost of motoring. But the point of a just transition is that it is a *transition* – although the need to have a radically altered transport system could not be more urgent, of necessity it will take time. Many people will still need to drive until we can fix the transport system, and many of those people are on incomes too low to be able to bear a huge increase in transport costs. None of this is to deny that motor vehicle use has to drop at unprecedented scale and speed, but that change also has to decrease socio-economic inequalities, not make them worse. An important part of that – albeit just a part – is to make public transport much more affordable.[74]

Innovative new services

A just transition also means thinking about how railways can provide services for people who usually fly, given that zero-carbon flying is not currently possible. The amount of carbon dioxide emitted through flying depends on the distance travelled. While domestic and short-haul flights emit more carbon dioxide on a per-kilometre basis, long-haul flights are responsible for the majority of aviation carbon emissions.[75] There is little that rail policy can do about that problem, which will need to be tackled through reduced travelling, at least in the short term. But where railways do come into their own is in offering an alternative to domestic and short-haul flights, which have to be dramatically reduced as well.

Clearly, reducing domestic and short-haul flights means improving the existing intercity network, with higher-capacity rolling stock alongside affordable fares. But it also means introducing new kinds of service which can make up for some of the loss of convenience from greatly reduced short-haul flying.

In mainland Europe, there has recently been a remarkable renaissance in overnight sleeper trains. The European sleeper network used to be very extensive, with overnight trains from nearly every major European city to almost every other. But they have been severely cut back in the last thirty or so years, owing to a mixture of high-speed day trains and cheap flights stealing passengers. Their recent re-emergence appears to be a result of passengers demanding their return because of fears of climate breakdown.[76] Night trains are the ultimate solution to the problem of how to get people off short-haul flights, because they make use of time that is usually 'wasted' sleeping, carrying you and your dreams hundreds of miles across the land.

Such a resurgence is yet to be seen in Britain, and is unlikely without significant public investment. All that remains of a sleeper network which once touched every major city and region in Britain are two services from London to Scotland and one from London to Penzance. Unsurprisingly, these are even more expensive to use than daytime trains. At the time of writing, a ticket booked a month ahead for a sleeper return from London to Aberdeen costs £450, as compared with £80 for a return by plane from London Gatwick. Indeed, British sleepers are increasingly marketed as 'train hotels', targeting the premium end of the tourist market rather than providing an everyday public transport alternative to flying.

The revival of the sleeper network should be at the heart of government policy, and should also include services to Europe. One of the last great ideas of BR was the 'Nightstar' – a fleet of sleeper coaches that was to be used in the newly built Channel Tunnel. Overnight services from London to cities in the Netherlands and Germany, and from Glasgow, Plymouth and Swansea to Paris and Brussels, with stops in between, were planned. BR got as far as ordering 139 specially built carriages, but privatisation and a rapid rise of low-cost airlines got in the way of the plans, and the government eventually sold the carriages to Canadian state railways at a huge discount.[77]

Safety

Finally, if the railways are going to attract people away from cars, they need to feel safe. This means not only maintaining and improving staffing levels, but also addressing the concerns that Covid-19 has raised. The dip in rail use as a result of Covid-19 was not just a result of millions of people getting used to working from home – it was also encouraged by strong government messaging, which urged people to avoid public transport. While this was sensible advice in the teeth of a pandemic and before the widespread rollout of vaccines, the government has done little to restore confidence in the safety of rail travel since the economy has reopened. At the time of writing, it is unknown whether repeated vaccine boosts will be enough to see off the threats of Covid-19 in the long term. Regardless, the risk of future epidemics – and people's awareness of the dangers of airborne viruses – are considerable.[78] Most modern rolling stock is air-conditioned, so it doesn't have opening windows. But there is still a lot that could be done to improve ventilation, by adjusting air-conditioning systems to pump more fresh air into carriages.[79] Unfortunately, there is little sign that such work is taking place.[80]

Of course, as has been argued in this book, a safe railway is a well-staffed railway. Every train should have at least two members of staff, including one to look after passengers. A just transition also means making the network fully accessible by eliminating the huge number of stations without level boarding through the installation of lifts and ramps.

Can we afford it?

The extent of public funding required to for the railways to enable a just transition would depend on the mix of measures taken up by a National Climate Service. Yet whatever these were, they would surely entail a much greater expenditure on public transport than has hitherto been undertaken.

The cost of the proposal above to regulate rail fares at half the cost of driving depends on how expensive driving becomes. In theory, fares could stay the same if road pricing massively increases the cost of motoring, but that is a political impossibility because it would very quickly impoverish most of the population. If rail fares were regulated according to a just transition, one would expect price incentives to work by making train travel much more affordable, rather than massively increasing the cost of driving.[81] Something of the order of the £22 billion a year subsidy that the railways received during the initial Covid-19 lockdowns would probably be required to be maintained in perpetuity in order to fund significant fare cuts, even with the much increased passenger numbers that a just transition would produce.[82] That this amount would have been smaller without years of privatisation is almost irrelevant, except for the fact that further privatisation would make a very difficult proposition impossible, because it would only increase costs and decrease organisational coherence. Much of the money required would be for operational and infrastructure staff. The war on Britain's railway workers would need to come to an end. Only cooperation and mutual trust would allow the rapid creation of a railway system fit for a just transition, including mechanisms to allow ordinary workers a much greater opportunity to have a say in the way the railways are run, and guaranteed jobs and retraining on the railways for those workers laid off from the car manufacturing and aviation industries.

If this all seems very unaffordable, consider the fact that within the last fifteen years, huge sums of public money have been found to stave off economic collapse, first as a response to the 2008 banking crisis and secondly during the Covid-19 pandemic.[83] A just transition would need to ensure that those with the broadest shoulders have the responsibility for paying for it.

Given the massive scale of public expenditure needed to implement decarbonisation and tackle inequality, there are growing calls for a 'wealth tax'. Wealth inequality in Britain has increased dramatically over the past forty years,[84] driven by tax cuts for the rich, and by increases in asset prices (especially housing and shares), which have occurred despite the banking and Covid-19 crises. Today, the richest top 20 per cent of individuals in the UK own 68.4 per cent of the wealth, while the bottom 20 per cent own just 0.4 per cent.[85] Recent research by academics at the Wealth Tax Commission estimates that the imposition of a one-off 1 per cent tax on individuals with wealth over £500,000 would raise £260 billion over five years. What is more, because it would be a one-off tax, each taxpayer's liability would already be fixed, meaning that the wealthy would have little opportunity to avoid paying it. This would go a significant way to raising much of the money needed to get the infrastructure projects necessary to start a just transition. An ongoing yearly wealth tax would also be required, although the imposition of the first, one-off tax would buy time to reform the international taxation system in order to close off tax-avoidance loopholes.[86]

Some of the money required could be found within the transport system itself. To give just one example, in 2021 the UK government provided a 50 per cent discount on air passenger duty for domestic flights, at a cost of £275 million.[87] This was funded by creating a new, higher duty on very long-haul flights. A tax on long-haul flights is a good idea, but to spend the proceeds on attempting to increase demand for domestic flights goes against decarbonisation efforts. Almost unbelievably, the air duty cut was the result of a recommendation by Sir Peter Hendy, chair of Network Rail – one of the bodies that is supposed to provide leadership for the rail industry.[88] Domestic air travel, already struggling with low profitability, got into even greater trouble during the first waves of Covid-19, and regional airports have been threatened with closure. For Hendy, it is vital to save the domestic aviation industry, which he believes provide services where 'journeys are too long to be reasonably taken by road or rail'.[89] Such is the lack of imagination and frivolous attitude to the climate emergency of Britain's railway leaders.

Of course, you have to look at the costs of *not* making the required changes as well. Traditional ways of valuing public spending are failing us. Spending is allocated according to a calculation of the costs versus the benefits of particular schemes. However, 90 per cent of the benefits accounted for in cost–benefit analyses in transport projects are for the time savings of individuals, on the assumption that time spent travelling is time that is wasted. In addition, the environmental impacts of schemes are heavily discounted in the calculations.[90] So what we end up with are schemes to speed up travel, which are mostly projects to reduce road congestion through increased motor vehicle capacity but also include high speed rail expansion. Although the UK government has declared a climate emergency, this has had little effect on how transport projects are evaluated. The brutal truth of the matter is that unless we immediately begin to make deep cuts in carbon dioxide emissions – which would involve a steep decline in car driving and flying, and a steep increase in zero-carbon transport such as electric trains, electric buses and bikes – runaway climate change is inevitable, and, before we know it, there will be no economy to speak of, because the natural earth systems which support it will have completely collapsed.

There are no guarantees that radically reforming all aspects of the economy – including transport – will successfully avert climate collapse, but the best available scientific evidence says that we have a chance if we throw everything we have at it, and similar efforts are made globally. And one thing's for certain: business as usual is over. Even if the decarbonisation of transport is not ultimately successful, the changes needed to get close to success would nevertheless be of massive benefit to society in terms of better connectivity and poverty reduction.

How do we get it?

Despite the logical and scientifically sound arguments for radically reforming our transport system, decades of inaction over climate change and transport poverty make it clear that being right is not enough: those who want to see radical reform will have to make it happen. Of course, this task reaches far beyond the railways, requiring big changes in the political landscape. For a just transition to occur, huge amounts of wealth and resources will need to be redistributed from the very wealthy to the rest of us. That will occur neither spontaneously nor with the consent of those to be dispossessed of their riches. History tells us that sudden and fundamental political changes occur only as a result of mass movements. A mass movement to force real and proportionate action on the climate emergency is needed.[91] The 2019 election witnessed a heavy defeat for the Labour Party, which had rail renationalisation as a cornerstone policy, not because renationalisation isn't popular, but because the overall political landscape was fixated on questions of nationhood and constitution. Despite a recent uptick in an environmentalist movement which is increasingly incorporating social demands into its activities, it is on nothing like the scale, and does not possess sufficient levels of power, to force a just transition to the top of the political agenda.

Successful mass movements win according to a few simple demands (for example 'votes for women', 'end apartheid' and 'stop the war'), but, when looked at in more detail, they contain a number of different organisations and currents that campaign on more specific issues within the broader movement.[92] Such is the potential for public transport campaigning as part of a mass movement for a just transition.

As we saw in Chapter 4, there have been examples of movements of railway passengers that have forced the industry to make changes that it didn't want to make. These have been too limited in terms of demands and scale to make much of a dent in overall rail policy. But there have also been examples where activists have fused campaigns over the railways and other forms of public transport, highlighted the social injustices of cuts and privatisation, worked with non-transport campaigning organisations such as trade unionists and community groups and used militant tactics such as fare strikes. Their successes provide inspiration for what will be required on a grander scale.

Furthermore, despite the fact that one of the purposes of privatisation was to reduce staffing costs by undermining the organisational abilities of rail trade unions, rail workers have been remarkably successful in defending themselves from the worst of attacks on them. Yet their strength has been predicated on a growing demand for rail services in the past thirty years, and the recent decline in commuting seems to have brought that to an end. Strikes can create significant economic disruption when services are very busy, but are far less powerful when bringing lightly loaded services to a standstill. So, whereas until recently rail unions could be highly effective while sticking to the more bread-and-butter trade unionist practices of striking and negotiation, they now also need to look to ways to bolster passenger numbers if they want to retain the bargaining power necessary to maintain a decent standard of living for their members. So becoming much more visible in climate change activism would seem a sensible course of action, because it is really only in the climate emergency context that the huge levels of government money required to significantly increase passenger numbers can be justified.

In short, it is up to passengers and railway workers to ensure that we can have a railway system that meets the exacting demands of a just transition. Success is far from guaranteed, but the railway industry and government policy elite, having presided over years of chaos, cost escalation and strife in order to make privatisation work, are fresh out of ideas.

Now is the time to seize on their ideological and moral bank-ruptcy, but we cannot do so by using tired clichés and replaying old battles. Seductive slogans like 'renationalise the railways' mean little to the younger generation of climate activists, who have forced 'net zero' onto the agenda and never knew the patch-it-and-mend misery of the state railway system. Almost anything would be better than the disaster the past two decades of privatisation have inflicted on passengers, but we cannot go back. The world is in a state of multiple and interrelated crises. Given that, perhaps the most dif-ficult thing of all is to pull away from day-to-day survival and to use the power of imagination to get from where we are to where we want to be. To do so involves courage, conviction and mutual support. We have to teach ourselves and learn from each other, and this book is an attempt to begin that process. That process will also need to involve new organisational spaces and forms, where passengers, rail workers and social justice and environmental activists can come together to strategise and debate. If we don't dream big and campaign for a rail system that genuinely meets our collective needs, then we sacrifice that political space to the financialising, asset-stripping, union-smashing, fare-increasing and passenger-criminalising cabal who have ruled railway policy, management and ownership for decades. We must fight like hell for rail system we all need and deserve.

All change please

It's 00:35. Exhausted and hungry, I am one of the last off the train. Its passengers form a bedraggled swarm, limping towards the ticket barriers, roller cases in tow. As I wait for the crowds to clear, my eyes are drawn upwards to huge iron girders that support the massive curved roof of Manchester Piccadilly station, still keeping passengers dry 160 years after its construction. Sitting atop are panes of glass – replacements for air vents that used to allow steam engines' smoke to dissipate into the wet Lancastrian sky.

When Manchester Piccadilly was built, the railways were icons of progress, celebrated by industrialists and romantic artists alike. A growing railway system promised a bright future of progress and material abundance. Now, unless we fix what's left of it, there *is* no future.

Notes

Introduction

1 See Leigh Shaw-Taylor and Xuesheng You, 'The Development of the Railway Network in Britain 1825–1911', in *The Online Historical Atlas of Transport, Urbanization and Economic Development in England and Wales c.1680–1911*, edited by Leigh Shaw-Taylor, Dan Bogart and Max Satchell, chap. 3, Cambridge University, https://www.geog.cam.ac.uk/research/projects/transport/onlineatlas/ (accessed 14 March 2022).

2 See Jean Shaoul, 'Railpolitik: A Stakeholder Analysis of the Railways' (University of Manchester, 1999), 10–11.

3 See Michael Bonavia, *British Railway Policy between the Wars* (Manchester University Press, 1981).

4 Terry Gourvish, *British Railways 1948–1973: A Business History* (Cambridge University Press, 1986), 1; Shaoul, 'Railpolitik', 11.

5 See Bonavia, *Railway Policy*; Gourvish, *British Railways 1948–1973*; Shaoul, 'Railpolitik', 11–12.

6 British Railways was formed as part of the larger British Transport Commission but became a standalone body in 1962.

7 See Shaoul, 'Railpolitik', 13; Andrew Bowman et al., *The Great Train Robbery: Rail Privatisation and After* (Centre for Research on Socio-Cultural Change, 2013), 135.

8 See Bowman et al., *The Great Train Robbery*, 135.

9 Harold Watkinson, cited in Charles Loft, 'Reappraisal and Reshaping: Government and the Railway Problem 1951–64', *Contemporary British History* 15, no. 4 (2001): 71–92, doi: 10.1080/713999426.

10 Christian Wolmar, *On the Wrong Line: How Ideology and Incompetence Wrecked Britain's Railways* (Kemsing, 2012), chap. 2, Kindle.

11 HM Government, *The British Transport Commission: Revised Draft of the White Paper* (National Archives, 1956), http://filestore.nationalarchives. gov.uk/pdfs/small/cab-129-83-cp-56-210-10.pdf (accessed 15 March 2022).

12 Wolmar, *On the Wrong Line*, chap. 2.

13 Ibid.

14 Ibid.

15 Gourvish, *British Railways 1948–1973*, 398; Wolmar, *On the Wrong Line*, chap. 2.

16 Wolmar, *On the Wrong Line*, chap. 2.

17 Terry Gourvish, 'British Rail's "Business-Led" Organization, 1977–1990: Government–Industry Relations in Britain's Public Sector', *Business History Review* 64, no. 1 (1990): 109–149 (122), doi: 10.2307/3115846; Bowman et al., *The Great Train Robbery*, 137.

18 Gourvish, 'British Rail's "Business-Led" Organization'.

19 Bowman et al., *The Great Train Robbery*.

20 Gourvish, 'British Rail's "Business-Led" Organization', 130.

21 Subsidy was reduced, in 1982 prices, from £933.4 million to £475.5 million. Author's calculation based on data from Terry Gourvish, *British Rail 1974–97: From Integration to Privatisation* (Oxford University Press, 2002), 455–456.

22 BRB and ITS (Leeds), cited in Gourvish, 'British Rail's "Business-Led" Organization', 149.

23 Bowman et al., *The Great Train Robbery*, 138.

24 John Shaw, *Competition, Regulation and the Privatisation of British Rail* (Ashgate, 2000). See also the appendix by John Major in Wolmar, *On the Wrong Line*.

Chapter 1

1 Data from European Commission rail market monitoring. See 'Rail Market Monitoring (RMMS)', European Commission, https://transport. ec.europa.eu/transport-modes/rail/market/rail-market-monitoring-rmms_ en (accessed 15 March 2022). Note that the UK figures may include the separate Northern Ireland Railways system, whose very small network would make very little difference to the overall UK figures. Note also that this is a cross-EU comparison, and so does not include non-EU countries

such as Switzerland, and that because of Brexit more recent figures for the UK are not available.

2 In calculating this figure, the methodology first employed by the National Audit Office has been used. The National Audit Office found that the average train creates £73.47 worth of economic loss for each minute of delay, based on government economic appraisal techniques of lost economic activity for different types of passenger. This methodology is explained in more detail in the report's appendices. See National Audit Office, *Reducing Passenger Rail Delays by Better Management of Incidents* (Stationery Office, 2008), https://webarchive.nationalarchives.gov.uk/uk gwa/20170207052351/https://www.nao.org.uk/wp-content/uploads/2008/03/0708308.pdf (accessed 15 March 2022). The National Audit Office multiplied this figure by the total number of passenger minutes lost in 2006/07 to reach an economic impact figure of £1.03 billion. I have updated this figure by taking the total number of minutes' delay for 2019/20 (17,060,120) from the Office of Rail and Road's data portal and multiplying it by £89.76 – the ORR's average economic impact of a minute's delay to a passenger service, inflated to 2019/20 prices using the Treasury's GDP deflators. See Office of Rail and Road, *Passenger Rail Performance*, https://dataportal.orr.gov.uk/statistics/performance/passenger-rail-performance/ (accessed 15 March 2022).

3 'Council Worker Lost his Job after Train Chaos Made him Late Three Days in a Row', *Express*, 2 June 2016, https://www.express.co.uk/news/uk/676219/council-worker-lost-job-atrain-chaos-made-him-late-three-days-row (accessed 15 March 2022).

4 Dean Kirby, 'Rail Commuters Are Moving House to Avoid Nightmare Train Cancellations and Delays', *iNews*, 25 January 2019, https://inews.co.uk/news/rail-commuters-are-moving-house-to-avoid-nightmare-train-cancellations-and-delays-250118 (accessed 15 March 2022).

5 Particularly trains other than the famous Shinkansen ('bullet train') high-speed services, which are almost entirely separated from other traffic. See Taku Fujiyama, 'Comparing Railway Systems in the UK and Japan from the View of their Punctuality', paper presented at the Daiwa Foundation Seminar, 22 May, 2018, Daiwa Foundation, https://dajf.org.uk/wp-content/uploads/Daiwa-Seminar.pdf (accessed 15 March 2022). A summary of the presentation is also available in Keith Fender, 'Punctuality Tokyo Style', *Modern Railways*, 24 January 2019, https://www.modernrailways.com/article/punctuality-tokyo-style (accessed 15 March 2022).

6 As in the question 'does the flap of a butterfly's wings in Brazil set off a tornado in Texas?' See Edward Lorenz, 'Predictability: Does the Flap of a Butterfly's Wings in Brazil Set Off a Tornado in Texas', paper presented to the American Association for the Advancement of Science, 139th Meeting, Cambridge, MA, 29 December 1972.

7 'How a Delay to Services in One Area Can Affect Trains Elsewhere in the Country', Network Rail, https://www.networkrail.co.uk/running-the-railway/looking-after-the-railway/delays-explained/knock-on-delays/ (accessed 15 March 2022).

8 Around two thirds of journeys are for commuting or business purposes. The remaining third are for leisure purposes. See 'Rail Passenger Numbers and Crowding on Weekdays in Major Cities in England and Wales: 2017', Department for Transport, https://assets.publishing.service.gov. uk/government/uploads/system/uploads/attachment_data/file/728526/rai l-passengers-crowding-2017.pdf (accessed 15 March 2022). However, this does not mean that all of the leisure journeys are non-discretionary – seeing friends and family or going on holiday is not a 'nice to have'.

9 Calculated from data in Department for Transport statistics, Table RAI0210. See 'Statistics at DfT', Department for Transport, https://www. gov.uk/government/statistical-data-sets/raio2-capacity-and-overcrowding (accessed 15 March 2022). The data shows the percentage of passengers in excess of capacity across both morning and evening three-hour peaks for all London and South-East operators. The data is expressed in terms of 'passengers in excess of capacity', a measurement of when a train is 'full', which provides an allowance for some standing, depending on the type of rolling stock being used. As the data table advises, comparisons across time should be treated cautiously, given changes in measurements. Indeed, a recent report by the House of Commons Transport Committee has criticised this official measurement of overcrowding. Cancelled trains are incorrectly included in the statistics, 'short-formed' services (services run with fewer carriages or units than planned) are taken out of overall capacity estimations, and overcrowding calculations are based on all train operating company services, not on routes. Each decision in terms of what to include and not to include in the data serves to under-estimate the problem of overcrowding and thus regulatory response to it. See House of Commons Transport Committee, *Overcrowding on Public Transport* (Stationery Office, 2003), https://publications.parliament.uk/ pa/cm200203/cmselect/cmtran/201/201.pdf (accessed 15 March 2022).

The committee's report also criticises official figures for only focussing on London and the south-east. This was later remedied from 2011 (see Department for Transport, rail statistics Table RAI0209 in 'Statistics at DfT', Department for Transport); however, that is of little use for those wishing to look at longer-term trends.

10 As reports attest. See, for example, London Assembly Transport Committee, *The Big Squeeze: Rail Overcrowding in London* (Greater London Authority, 2009), https://www.london.gov.uk/sites/default/files/gla_migrate_files_destination/archives/FINAL_Overcrowding_report.pdf; Avril Campbell, 'Overcrowded Trains on Edinburgh to North Berwick Railway Line "at Breaking Point"', *East Lothian Courier*, 7 April 2016, https://www.eastlothiancourier.com/news/14408077.overcrowded-trains-on-edinburgh-to-north-berwick-railway-line-at-breaking-point/; Stephanie Balloo, 'Fury as Platforms Full of Commuters Left Stranded by Delayed and Overcrowded Trains', *Birmingham Live*, 2 April 2019, https://www.birminghammail.co.uk/news/midlands-news/fury-platforms-full-commuters-left-14367887; Ian Hughes, 'Over 100 Passengers Left Behind on Leeds to Manchester Trains Every Day Due to Overcrowding', *Leeds Live*, 23 September 2019, https://www.leeds-live.co.uk/news/leeds-news/over-100-passengers-left-behind-16963058; Katie-Ann Gupwell, 'Delays, Overcrowding, Cancellations Provoke Wave of Anger over Transport for Wales Services', *Wales Online*, 1 October 2019, https://www.walesonline.co.uk/news/wales-news/transport-for-wales-cardiff-anger-16991608; James Thomas, 'Passengers' Fury Mounts over Train Services', 3 February 2020, https://www.herefordtimes.com/news/18201500.passengers-fury-mounts-train-services/ (all websites accessed 15 March 2022).

11 Clive Charlton, 'The Structure of the New Railway', in *All Change: British Railway Privatisation*, edited by Roger Freeman and Jon Shaw (McGraw-Hill, 2000), 31–56 (43); Chris Nash, Simon Coulthard and Bryan Matthews, 'Rail Track Charges in Great Britain – The Issue of Charging for Capacity', *Transport Policy* 11, no. 4 (2004): 315–327.

12 John Edmonds, 'Creating Railtrack', in *All Change: British Railway Privatisation*, edited by Roger Freeman and Jon Shaw (McGraw-Hill, 2000), 57–81.

13 Shaw, *Competition, Regulation and the Privatisation of British Rail*; John Swift, 'The Role of the Rail Regulator', in *All Change: British Railway Privatisation*, edited by Roger Freeman and Jon Shaw (McGraw-Hill, 2000), 205–228.

14 As epitomised by the 'RPI minus x' formula that the Rail Regulator used to set Railtrack's income through track access charges in the first years of privatisation. Here, 'minus x' refers to a given amount that track access charges should be reduced by every year, and RPI refers to retail price index inflation. The formula assumes that charges must be reduced, and that a private company like Railtrack could still make a profit if faced with declining income, thanks to its private-sector ability to reduce costs. Since a good proportion of track access charges came from public subsidy, it was a technical expression of a political objective – to use privatisation to reduce public subsidy. For details of how Railtrack's regulatory system emerged see Edmonds, 'Creating Railtrack'; Arthur Leathley, 'Railtrack's Recent Performance', in *All Change: British Railway Privatisation*, edited by Roger Freeman and Jon Shaw (McGraw-Hill, 2000), 83–96; Shaw, *Competition, Regulation and the Privatisation of British Rail*; and Swift, 'The Role of the Rail Regulator'.

15 Calculated from Railtrack PLC annual reports and accounts, various years.

16 Robert Jupe and Gerald Crompton, 'Delivering Better Transport? An Evaluation of the Ten-Year Plan for the Railway Industry', *Public Money and Management* 22, no. 3 (2002): 41–48 (43), doi: 10.1111/1467-9302.00317.

17 K. Harper, 'Railtrack £17 Billion "Too Little"', *Guardian*, 26 March 1998, 21, as cited in Jupe and Crompton, 'Delivering Better Transport?', 43.

18 Cited in Gerald Crompton and Robert Jupe, '"Such a Silly Scheme": The Privatisation of Britain's Railways 1992–2002', *Critical Perspectives on Accounting* 14, no. 6 (2003): 617–645 (632), doi: 10.1016/S1045-2354(02)00187-9.

19 National Audit Office, *Ensuring that Railtrack Maintain and Renew the Railway Network* (Stationery Office, 2000), MC 397.

20 Office of Rail Regulation, *Train Derailment at Hatfield: A Final Report by the Independent Investigation Board*, Office of Rail Regulation, July 2006, https://web.archive.org/web/20130629070532/http://www.railwaysarchive.co.uk/documents/HSE_HatfieldFinal2006.pdf (accessed 15 March 2022).

21 Wolmar, *On the Wrong Line*.

22 'New Labour Because Britain Deserves Better', Labour Party, 1997, www.labour-party.org.uk/manifestos/1997/1997-labour-manifesto.shtml (accessed 15 March 2022).

23 Swift, 'The Role of the Rail Regulator', 210.

24 'A New Deal for Transport: Better for Everyone', Department for Transport, Local Government and Regions, https://www.railwaysarchive. co.uk/docsummary.php?docID=196 (accessed 15 March 2022).

25 Steve Melia, *Roads, Runways and Resistance: From the Newbury Bypass to Extinction Rebellion* (Pluto, 2021).

26 Ed Balls and Gus O'Donnell, *Reforming Britain's Economic and Financial Policy: Towards Greater Economic Stability* (Palgrave, 2002).

27 Robert Jupe, 'New Labour, Network Rail and the Third Way', *Accounting, Auditing & Accountability Journal* 22, no. 5 (2009): 709–735, doi: 10.1108/09513570910966342. Fine and Saad-Filho have characterised this kind of social policy as 'third wayist' and financialised social policy as being characteristic of neoliberalism. In their view, informed by Marxist political economy, financialisation involves the extensive and intensive growth of 'interest-bearing capital' – money which is advanced in the expectation of a return after intermediary productive processes – into new areas of the economy to support social and economic reproduction. Importantly, interest-bearing capital has a tendency to move away from real, underlying value in the economy, becoming 'fictitious capital', which accumulates until reaching a crisis point, whereby paper values are undermined. Arguably, the creation of Network Rail by New Labour was a large-scale experiment in working with international financial markets to create fictitious capital. As we will see, the results were disastrous. See Ben Fine and Alfredo Saad-Filho, 'Thirteen Things You Need to Know about Neoliberalism', *Critical Sociology* 43, nos 4–5 (2017): 685–706, doi: 10.1177/0896920516655387.

28 The company instead had 'members' who were the legal owners, but had very little say in the running of the company and had been installed to maintain the fiction of Network Rail not being an arm of government.

29 This figure was subsequently reduced to £21.45 billion by the Rail Regulator, following pressure from the government to reduce subsidy. See Terry Gourvish, *Britain's Railways 1997–2005: Labour's Strategic Experiment* (Oxford University Press, 2008), 193–196.

30 Interview with Tom Winsor (the then Rail Regulator), 14 May 2019. See also Gourvish, *Britain's Railways 1997–2005*, 189–201.

31 Interview with Tom Winsor, 14 May 2019.

32 According to Gourvish, the proportion of Network Rail's income allocated to borrowing was initially 15 per cent, with the rest of the income coming from government grants, and track access charges paid by train operating companies. Gourvish, *Britain's Railways 1997–2005*, 196. However, as we shall see, the interest burden of Network Rail's borrowing quickly began

to mount, meaning much greater amounts of additional borrowing over time.

33 Note in Figure 1.3 that infrastructure spending is reported as 'capital expenditure' and 'other external charges' in accounts. The latter category may include some spending that is not directly for infrastructure maintenance, but infrastructure maintenance represents the overwhelming majority of Railtrack's and Network Rail's expenditure in that accounting category, as illustrated in the handful of accounts which indicate what proportion of 'other external charges' represent maintenance expenditure. Inflation calculated using the Office for National Statistics GDP deflator tables.

34 Office of Rail and Road statistics, Tables 1220 and 3103. See 'Welcome to the ORR Data Portal', Office of Rail and Road, https://dataportal.orr.gov.uk/ (accessed 15 March 2022).

35 Roger Ford, 'Informed Sources', *Modern Railways*, December 2015, http://live.ezezine.com/ezine/pdf/759-2015.11.23.04.00.archive.pdf (accessed 15 March 2022).

36 Bowman et al., *The Great Train Robbery*, 25.

37 Gill Plimmer and Jim Pickard, 'Network Rail Debt Move Goes Off Track', *Financial Times*, 12 August 2014, https://www.ft.com/content/fc31718c-156a-11e4-ae2e-00144feabdc0 (accessed 15 March 2022).

38 'What Reclassification Means for Investors', Network Rail, https://www.networkrail.co.uk/industry-and-commercial/third-party-investors/debt-investor-relations/information-for-investors/what-reclassification-means-for-investors/ (accessed 15 March 2022).

39 In Figure 1.4, figures for 1985/86–2018/19 are from Office of Rail and Road statistics, Table 1.6. Figures for 2019/20–2020/21 are from Table 7270. In effect, Table 7270 replaced Table 1.6. The latter includes what was formally accounted for as government loans to Network Rail in subsidy figures. Table 1.6 remains available on request from the Office of Rail and Road. Note that freight grants are accounted for separately in Table 1.6 but not in Table 7270. To ensure consistency of data, freight grants are assumed to be an element of government subsidy to the railways in the figures presented here. Figures adjusted to inflation using the Office for National Statistics GDP deflator tables. Subsidy figures include annual spending on new projects, including Crossrail and HS2.

40 Interview with Patrick Butcher, 8 March 2018.

41 Peter Hendy, *Report from Sir Peter Hendy to the Secretary of State for Transport on the Replanning of Network Rail's Investment Programme*

(Network Rail, 2015), https://www.networkrail.co.uk/wp-content/uploa ds/2019/06/hendy-report.pdf (accessed 15 March 2022).

42 Calculated from figures in Office of Rail and Road statistics, Table 3184, based on an annual average from 2011/15 to 2019/20, with 2020/21 excluded because of the exceptional nature of the year. See 'Welcome to the ORR Data Portal', Office of Rail and Road.

43 As the managing director of one of the main train operating companies testified before parliament. See House of Commons Committee of Public Accounts, *Reducing Passenger Rail Delays by Better Management of Incidents* (Stationery Office, 2008), https://publications.parliament.uk/ pa/cm200708/cmselect/cmpubacc/655/655.pdf (accessed 15 March 2022).

44 See, for example, 'Southern Railway Confirms 341 Trains Per Day will be Axed in New Timetable', *Surrey Live*, 11 July 2016, https://www.getsurrey. co.uk/news/surrey-news/southern-railway-confirms-341-trains-11568742; Sean Morrison, 'Gatwick Express Claim that Trains to Victoria Take "Just 30 Minutes" Ruled as Misleading', *Evening Standard*, 31 July 2018, https://www.standard.co.uk/news/transport/gatwick-express-must-stop-c laiming-trains-to-victoria-take-just-30-minutes-after-fifth-of-trains-delaye d-a3900936.html; Adam Postans, 'Great Western Railway Boss Publicly Apologises for Train Delays but Warns More Still to Come', *Bristol Live*, 7 March 2019, https://www.bristolpost.co.uk/news/bristol-news/bristol- temple-meads-train-delays-2620492; 'Northern and Transpennine Rail Delays as New Timetable Begins', *BBC News*, 16 December 2019, https:// www.bbc.co.uk/news/uk-england-leeds-50807987 (all websites accessed 15 March 2022).

45 Author's calculations, based on data in Office of Rail and Road statistics, Table 3184, covering the years 2014/15 to 2020/21. See 'Welcome to the ORR Data Portal', Office of Rail and Road.

46 Author's calculations from figures presented in Office of Rail and Road statistics, Table 7226. See 'Welcome to the ORR Data Portal', Office of Rail and Road.

47 Tim Strangleman, *Work Identity at the End of the Line? Privatisation and Culture Change in the UK Rail Industry* (Palgrave Macmillan, 2004), 148.

48 Tanya Powley, '"Northern Powerhouse" in £1.2bn Rail Upgrade Boost', *Financial Times*, 9 December 2015, https://www.ft.com/content/7195305a- 9e4d-11e5-8ce1-f6219b685d74 (accessed 15 March 2022).

49 Network Rail, cited in House of Commons Transport Committee, *Rail Timetable Changes: May 2018* (Stationery Office, 4 December 2018), 5,

https://publications.parliament.uk/pa/cm201719/cmselect/cmtrans/1163/1 163.pdf (accessed 15 March 2022).

50   Powley, '"Northern Powerhouse"'.

51   Network Rail, *Railway Upgrade Plan 2017/18* (Network Rail, 2017), 22, https://www.networkrail.co.uk/wp-content/uploads/2017/08/Railway-U pgrade-Plan-Update-2017-2018.pdf (accessed 15 March 2022).

52   Department for Transport and Patrick McLoughlin, 'Better Journeys for Rail Customers as New Northern and Transpennine Express Franchises Confirmed' (Department for Transport, 23 December 2015), https://www. gov.uk/government/news/better-journeys-for-rail-customers-as-new-nor thern-and-transpennine-express-franchises-confirmed (accessed 15 March 2022).

53   House of Commons Transport Committee, *Rail Timetable Changes*, 6; Office of Rail and Road, *Office of Rail and Road: Independent Inquiry into the Timetable Disruption in May 2018* (Office of Rail and Road, 2018), 7, https://www.orr.gov.uk/sites/default/files/om/inquiry-into-may-2018- timetable-disruption-september-2018-findings.pdf (accessed 15 March 2022).

54   These figures exclude additional disruption caused by strike action at this time. House of Commons Transport Committee, *Rail Timetable Changes*, 7. See Chapter 3 below.

55   Janina Conboye and Andy Bounds, 'Northern Rail Woes Lasted Long after Timetable Debacle, Regulator Finds', *Financial Times*, 27 June 2019, https://www.ft.com/content/d2da584e-98be-11e9-8cfb-30c211dcd229 (accessed 15 March 2022); Tim Gavell, 'Northern Agrees Deal with Aslef to Ease Blackpool's Weekend Train Cancellations Nightmare', *The Gazette*, 17 January 2020, https://www.manchestereveningnews.co.uk/ news/greater-manchester-news/northern-rail-cancellations-unions-drivers -17742818 (accessed 15 March 2022).

56   House of Commons Transport Committee, *Rail Timetable Changes*, 13–14.

57   Gary Bogan, cited in ibid., 13.

58   House of Commons Transport Committee, 'Oral Evidence: Rail Timetable Changes', HC 1163 (Stationery Office, 18 June 2018), question 18, https://data.parliament.uk/writtenevidence/committeeevidence.svc/ evidencedocument/transport-committee/rail-timetable-changes/oral/857 54.htm (accessed 15 March 2022); Office of Rail and Road, *Independent Inquiry*.

59   Office of Rail and Road, *Independent Inquiry*.

60   House of Commons Transport Committee, *Rail Timetable Changes*, 22.

61   Michael Savage, 'Is This the Best we can Do with Britain's Railways?', *Guardian*, 7 January 2018, https://www.theguardian.com/uk-news/2018/jan/07/britains-railways-is-this-the-best-we-can-do-renationalisation-strikes-fare-rises; 'MPs' Group Backs Plan for New Rail "Guiding Mind"', *Railnews*, 7 November 2019, https://www.railnews.co.uk/news/2019/11/07-mps-group-backs-plan-for.html; 'A Rational New Model for Britain's Railways', *Financial Times*, 20 May 2021, https://www.ft.com/content/0b0a0d0e-e418-4346-84f6-eabefa099fd6; Mark Walker, 'Williams–Shapps Plan for Rail – Evidence Session by the House of Commons Transport Committee: Summary Report and Analysis', *Cogitamus*, 26 May 2021, https://cogitamus.co.uk/wp-content/uploads/2021/05/No.-2-House-of-Commons-Transport-Committee-Hearing-Summary-Report-and-Analysis-270521.pdf (all websites accessed 15 March 2022).

62   See also Chapter 3.

63   Antoni Verger, Clara Fontdevil and Adrián Zancajo, The Privatization of Education: A Political Economy of Global Education Reform (Teachers College Press, 2016); Youssef El-Gingihy, *How to Dismantle the NHS in 10 Easy Steps: The Blueprint that the Government Does Not Want You to See* (John Hunt, 2018); Bob Hudson, *Clients, Consumers or Citizens? The Privatisation of Adult Social Care in England* (Policy Press, 2021).

Chapter 2

1   According to the Transport Focus Data Hub. See 'Transport Focus Data Hub', Transport Focus, https://transportfocusdatahub.org.uk (accessed 15 March 2022).

2   British fares taken from brfares.com, German fares from Bahn.com. See 'BR Fares', https://www.brfares.com/; 'Cheap Train Tickets', Deutsche Bahn, https://www.bahn.de/. German fares based on two Flexpreis singles (returns not being available in Germany), added together and converted into pounds sterling using xe.com. See 'Currency Exchange Rates', https://www.xe.com/ (all websites accessed 15 March 2022).

3   See Passenger Focus, *Passenger Focus Response to the Government's Rail Fares and Ticketing Review* (Passenger Focus, June 2012), https://www.transportfocus.org.uk/publication/passenger-focus-response-to-the-governments-rail-fares-and-ticketing-review/ (accessed 15 March 2022). For

that study's methods, see Steer Davis Gleave, *Research Report: Comparisons between Fares and Ticketing in Great Britain and Continental Europe* (Steer Davis Gleave, February 2009), https://www.transportfocus.org.uk/publication/fares-and-ticketing-study-appendix-b-comparisons-between-fares-and-ticketing-in-great-britain-and-continental-europe/ (accessed 15 March 2022).

4 'Fares FAQs', Rail Delivery Group, https://www.raildeliverygroup.com/uk-rail-industry/about-my-journey/fares-explained/fares-faqs.html (accessed 15 March 2022).

5 See, for example, Guy Birchall, 'Find a Rail Bargain: Rail Fare Increase for 2018 – How to Save Money on UK Rail Journeys from Split-Tickets to Early Deals', *The Sun*, 1 January 2018, https://www.thesun.co.uk/news/1619874/train-fare-rises-2018-uk-rail-prices-tickets-deals/; Andy Bagnall, cited in Jonny Ball, 'Why are the UK's Trains So Expensive?', *New Statesman*, 13 August 2021, https://www.newstatesman.com/spotlight/2021/08/why-are-uks-trains-so-expensive; Kieran Murray, 'Northern Launches Flash Sale With Train Tickets up for Grabs from Just £1', *Chronicle Live*, 24 August 2021, https://www.chroniclelive.co.uk/news/north-east-news/northern-launches-flash-sale-train-21383504; David Hannant, 'How to Get from Norwich to London for Just a Fiver', *Norwich Evening News*, 11 October 2021, https://www.eveningnews24.co.uk/news/traffic/greater-anglia-five-pound-london-tickets-8401396 (all websites accessed 15 March 2022).

6 Claire Perry, cited in Ray Massey, 'So Where Exactly Are Those £15 Rail Fares, Minister? "Cheap Tickets" Hailed by Claire Perry are Impossible to Find', *Daily Mail*, 19 August 2015, https://www.dailymail.co.uk/news/article-3202888/So-exactly-15-rail-fares-minister-Cheap-tickets-hailed-Claire-Perry-impossible-find.html (accessed 15 March 2022).

7 Barry Doe, cited in House of Lords Built Environment Committee, *Corrected Oral Evidence: Williams–Shapps Plan for Rail – Fare Reform*, 13 July 2021, https://committees.parliament.uk/oralevidence/2569/pdf/ (accessed 15 March 2022).

8 According to the latest pre-Covid figures in Office of Rail and Road, *Passenger Rail Usage 2019–20 Q4* (Office for Rail and Road, 4 June 2020), https://dataportal.orr.gov.uk/media/1740/passenger-rail-usage-2019-20-q4.pdf (accessed 15 March 2022).

9 Nigel Harris and Ernest Godward, *The Privatisation of British Rail* (Railway Consultancy Press, 1997), 41–42.

10 This view is more clearly and succinctly expressed in Sir Christopher Foster's pamphlet on rail privatisation. See Christopher Foster, *The*

Economics of Rail Privatisation (Chartered Institute of Public Finance and Accountancy, 1994). Foster was a key advisor to the government during the privatisation process. See Robert Jupe and Warwick Funnell, 'Neoliberalism, Consultants and the Privatisation of Public Policy Formulation: The Case of Britain's Rail Industry', *Critical Perspectives on Accounting* 29 (2015): 65–85, doi: 10.1016/j.cpa.2015.02.001.

11 Shaw, *Competition, Regulation and the Privatisation of British Rail*, 159.

12 A report published by the Strategic Rail Authority in 2003 states that regulated fare income accounted for 46 per cent of total fare income. See Strategic Rail Authority, *Fares Review Conclusions 2003* (Strategic Rail Authority, 2003), https://www.orr.gov.uk/sites/default/files/om/sra-fares-conclusions-2003.pdf (accessed 15 March 2022). A House of Commons briefing paper published in 2018 puts this figure at 45 per cent: see Noel Dempsey, *Railways: Fares Statistics* (House of Commons Library, 30 November 2018), https://researchbriefings.files.parliament.uk/document s/SN06384/SN06384.pdf (accessed 15 March 2022).

13 Wolmar, *On the Wrong Line*, chap. 3.

14 John Preston and Dawn Robins, 'Evaluating the Long Term Impacts of Transport Policy: The Case of Passenger Rail Privatisation', *Research in Transportation Economics* 39, no. 1 (2013): 14–20 (16), doi: 10.1016/j. retrec.2012.05.019. Although the RPI is now not a useful way to calculate fare inflation, there was little difference between RPI and Consumer Prices Index measures at that time.

15 Strategic Rail Authority, *Fares Review Conclusions 2003*, 2, 3, 13.

16 Although government subsidy has substantially increased in absolute terms, thanks to the explosion of railway costs since then. The funding proportion changes are reported in Christian Wolmar, 'Christian Wolmar: Londoners Need Railways – Don't Price Us Off Them', *Evening Standard*, 19 August 2014, https://www.standard.co.uk/comment/chris tian-wolmar-londoners-need-railways-don-t-price-us-off-them-9678464. html (accessed 15 March 2022). GB rail industry financial information, published on the Office of Rail and Road's data portal, shows that, roughly speaking, this proportion has been upheld by government policy for at least the last decade. See 'Rail Industry Finance (UK)', Office of Rail and Road, https://dataportal.orr.gov.uk/statistics/finance/rail-indus try-finance/#:~:text=Total%20rail%20industry%20income%20in,1.3%20 billion%20from%20other%20sources (accessed 15 March 2022).

17 See 'Shortcomings of the Retail Prices Index as a Measure of Inflation', Office for National Statistics, https://www.ons.gov.uk/economy/

inflationandpriceindices/articles/shortcomingsoftheretailpricesindexasam
easureofinflation/2018-03-08 (accessed 15 March 2022). See also 'Dataset: Consumer Prices Index Including Owner Occupiers' Housing Costs (CPIH)', Office for National Statistics, https://www.ons.gov.uk/datasets/cpih01/editions/time-series/versions/13 (accessed 15 March 2022).

18 SPA Future Thinking, *Understanding and Testing Passenger Perceptions of Complexity in Relation to Fares and Ticketing* (SPA Future Thinking, October 2011), https://www.orr.gov.uk/media/10758/download (accessed 15 March 2022).

19 Passenger Focus, *Passenger Focus Response to the Government's Rail Fares and Ticketing Review* (Passenger Focus, June 2012), https://d3cez36w5wym xj.cloudfront.net/migrated/Passenger%20Focus%20response%20to%20th e%20rail%20fares%20and%20ticketing%20review%20-%20June%202012. pdf (accessed 15 March 2022).

20 Accent and PJM Economics, *The Demand Impact of Fares Structure Simplification – Advanced Fares* (Accent, 2016).

21 The names of these tickets have been changed over time.

22 As set out in the Ticketing and Settlement Agreement. Abellio East Anglia Limited et al., *Ticketing and Settlement Agreement*, vol. 1: *Main Agreement* (Rail Delivery Group, 2021), chap. 6, part 30.

23 As a recent report by the House of Commons Transport Committee has found. The committee was puzzled that the regulator had not forced train operating companies to make split ticketing options clearer. See House of Commons Transport Committee, *The Future of Rail: Improving the Rail Passenger Experience* (House of Commons, 10 October 2016), https://publications.parliament.uk/pa/cm201617/cmselec t/cmtrans/64/64.pdf (accessed 15 March 2022).

24 See 'RailUK Fares & Ticketing Guide', RailUK Forums, https://www.rail forums.co.uk/forums/railuk-fares-ticketing-guide.153 (accessed 15 March 2022).

25 Transport Focus, *Ticket to Ride? Full Report* (Transport Focus, May 2012), https://d3cez36w5wymxj.cloudfront.net/migrated/Ticket%20to%20 Ride%20–%20full%20report%20-%20May%202012%20-%20FINAL.pdf; Transport Focus, *Ticket to Ride – An Update* (Transport Focus, February 2015), https://d3cez36w5wymxj.cloudfront.net/migrated/Ticket%20to%2 0Ride%20%E2%80%93%20an%20update%20-%20February%202015%20 -%20FINAL.pdf; Transport Focus, *Penalty Fares – The Appeals Process* (Transport Focus, February 2020), https://d3cez36w5wymxj.cloudfront.

net/wp-content/uploads/2020/02/06113518/Penalty-fares-the-appeals-proc ess-V2.pdf (all websites accessed 15 March 2022).

26 Passenger Focus, *Penalty Fares*, 10.

27 Ibid.

28 Matt Rudd, 'Caught between Rolling Stock and a Hard Place', *The Times*, 1 April 2012, https://www.thetimes.co.uk/article/caught-between-rolling-stock-and-a-hard-place-whjptd9zqth (accessed 15 March 2022).

29 Passenger Focus, *Penalty Fares*, 15.

30 Rail Delivery Group, *Big Plan: Big Changes* (Rail Delivery Group, February 2019), https://bigplanbigchanges.co.uk/files/docs/Fares_reform_propos als_A4_WEB_DPS.pdf (accessed 15 March 2022).

31 'Rail Delivery Group Reiterates Call for Train Fare Reform', *Rail Business UK*, 1 March 2021, https://web.archive.org/web/20210304094907/ https://www.raildeliverygroup.com/about-us/priorities/fares-reform-pro posals/2110-media-centre/press-releases/2018/469774583-2018-09-10.html (accessed 15 March 2022); 'Nearly 20,000 People Respond to Fares Consultation', Rail Delivery Group, https://www.raildeliverygroup.com/ about-us/priorities/fares-reform-proposals/2110-media-centre/press-relea ses/2018/469774583-2018-09-10.html (accessed 15 March 2022).

32 Rail Delivery Group, cited in Tom Edgington, 'Reality Check: Where Does Your Train Fare Go?', *BBC News*, 30 November 2018, https://www. bbc.co.uk/news/business-46398947 (accessed 15 March 2022).

33 As confirmed by the author of the original unpublished research in email correspondence. Ben Condry, email to Thomas Haines-Doran, 21 September 2021.

34 Depending on calculation and year studied. The Rail Delivery Group's figure of 2p is somewhat lower than the figure of 3p to 5p cited in Jean Shaoul, 'Leasing Passenger Trains: The British Experience', *Transport Reviews* 27, no. 2 (2007): 189–212 (204), doi: 10.1080/0144164060090 7024.

35 Andrew Bowman et al., *The Conceit of Enterprise: Train Operators and the Trade Narrative* (Centre for Research on Socio-Cultural Change, 2013), https://hummedia.manchester.ac.uk/institutes/cresc/sites/default/files/G TR%20Report%20final%205%20June%202013.pdf (accessed 15 March 2022).

36 It is impossible to quantify these losses, but to give some indication of the levels, McCartney and Stittle found the extra costs attributable to privatisation to have been around £50 billion by 2013/14 (or £61 billion at 2021 prices). See Sean McCartney and John Stittle, '"A Very Costly

Industry": The Cost of Britain's Privatised Railway', *Critical Perspectives on Accounting* 49 (2017): 1–17, doi: 10.1016/j.cpa.2017.04.002. By contrast, before the Covid-19 crisis, annual fares and passenger income totalled £11.6 billion. See 'Rail Industry Finance (UK)', Office of Rail and Road.

37 BR did outsource some construction of rolling stock to private companies, but would own the stock once procured. See Shaoul, 'Leasing Passenger Trains'; Jupe and Funnell, 'Neoliberalism, Consultants'.

38 Sean McCartney and John Stittle, '"Engines of Extravagance": The Privatised British Railway Rolling Stock Industry', *Critical Perspectives on Accounting* 23, no. 2 (2012): 153–167, doi: 10.1016/j.cpa.2011.10.001.

39 Shaoul found this to be the case (see Shaoul, 'Leasing Passenger Trains', 191), as did the present author, who had a number of freedom of information requests regarding the rolling stock companies refused by the Department for Transport on a similar basis.

40 Ben Webster, 'Banks are Making "Excessive Profits" from Leasing Old Trains', *The Times*, 28 June 2006, www.thetimes.co.uk/article/banks-are-making-excessive-profits-from-leasing-old-trains-m3dm00bqw65 (accessed 15 March 2022).

41 According to the latest available information, from 2017. See Office of Rail and Road, *Rail Infrastructure and Assets 2018–19 Annual Statistical Release* (Office of Rail and Road, 7 November 2019), 11, https://dataportal.orr.gov.uk/media/1533/rail-infrastructure-assets-2018-19.pdf?#:~:text=Rolling%20stock%20leasing%20companies%20(ROSCOs,and%2011%25%20in%20March%202017 (accessed 15 March 2022).

42 National Union of Rail, Maritime and Transport Workers, *The ROSCO Racket: Why it's Time to Take Control of UK Rolling Stock* (National Union of Rail, Maritime and Transport Workers), https://www.rmt.org.uk/news/publications/the-rosco-racket-why-its-time-to-take-control-of-uk-rolling/the-rosco-racket-why-it-s-time-to-take-control-of-uk-rolling-stock.pdf (accessed 16 March 2022).

43 Office of Rail Regulation, *The Leasing of Rolling Stock for Franchised Passenger Services: Consultation on the Findings of ORR's Market Study and on a Draft Reference to the Competition Commission* (Office of Rail Regulation, 29 November 2006), https://webarchive.nationalarchives.gov.uk/ukgwa/20090707063046/http://www.rail-reg.gov.uk/upload/pdf/308.pdf (accessed 15 March 2022); Competition Commission, *Rolling Stock Leasing Market Investigation* (Competition Commission, 7 April 2009), https://webarchive.nationalarchives.gov.uk/20140403004006/http://www.competition-commission.org.uk/assets/competitioncommission/

docs/pdf/non-inquiry/rep_pub/reports/2009/fulltext/546.pdf (accessed 15 March 2022).

44 As the Competition Commission stated, the 'distorting effects' of regulation 'would have long-term adverse consequences in terms of limiting investment in existing rolling stock and new rolling stock and discouraging entry'. Competition Commission, *Rolling Stock*, 17. An early inquiry into railway finances by the Select Committee on Environment, Transport and Regional Affairs reports that Angel Trains (one of the 'big three' rolling stock companies, or ROSCOS) told it that further regulation would not be required because legislation 'would provide adequate protection against anti-competitive behaviour by the ROSCOs without jeopardising the availability of funds from the capital markets'. House of Commons Environment, Transport and Regional Affairs Committee, *Environment, Transport and Regional Affairs – Third Report* (Stationery Office, 1 March 1998), para. 80, https://publications.parliament.uk/pa/cm199798/cmselect/cmenvtra/286iii/et0302.htm (accessed 15 March 2022).

45 Moody's, *Rating Action: Moody's Affirms the Great Rolling Stock Company's Ratings* (Moody's, 20 October 2016); Moody's, *The Great Rolling Stock Company Limited: Annual Update to Credit Analysis* (Moody's, 21 December 2017); Tom Haines-Doran, interview with Andrew Blease and Tomas O'Loughlin of Moody's, 7 February 2018. See also 'TEXT-S&P summary: Willow BidCo Ltd.', *Reuters*, 21 September 2012, https://www.reuters.com/article/idINWLA36082012092I (accessed 15 March 2022).

46 Competition Commission, *Rolling Stock*, 3.

47 Under New Labour, the government did start procuring rolling stock directly for some intercity and regional stock. However, because these were public–private partnerships, they retained the principal problem of the rolling stock company model, namely wealth extraction by private financiers. See Julie Froud et al., *Knowing What to Do? How Not to Build Trains* (Centre for Research on Socio-Cultural Change, July 2011), https://hummedia.manchester.ac.uk/institutes/cresc/sites/default/files/Knowing%20what%20to%20do.pdf (accessed 15 March 2022).

48 Environmental Audit Committee, *Environmental Audit – Second Report* (Stationery Office, 28 February 2001), https://publications.parliament.uk/pa/cm200001/cmselect/cmenvaud/71/7104.htm (accessed 15 March 2022). It is unclear whether the inflation measure used in these budgets is the Consumer Prices Index or RPI. Either way, they represented significant increases in the price of motor fuels.

49 Antony Seely, *Taxation of Road Fuels: The Road Fuel Escalator (1993–2000)* (House of Commons Library, 21 January 2011), https://researchbriefings. files.parliament.uk/documents/SN03015/SN03015.pdf (accessed 15 March 2022).

50 HM Treasury, *Budget 2001* (Stationery Office, March 2001), https://assets. publishing.service.gov.uk/government/uploads/system/uploads/attachme nt_data/file/266041/hc279.pdf (accessed 15 March 2022); Seely, *Taxation of Road Fuels*.

51 Campaign for Better Transport, *Written Evidence Submitted by Campaign for Better Transport* (Environment Audit Committee, 7 July 2011), https://publications.parliament.uk/pa/cm201012/cmselect/ cmenvaud/878/878we02.htm (accessed 15 March 2022).

52 Carl Emmerson, Christine Farquharson and Paul Johnson, eds, *The IFS Green Budget* (Institute for Fiscal Studies, October 2019), 221, https://ifs. org.uk/uploads/The-2019-IFS-Green-Budget-Updated-2.pdf (accessed 15 March 2022).

53 Department for Business, Energy & Industrial Strategy, Digest of UK Energy Statistics, Table 3B. Obtained through correspondence with Department for Business, Energy & Industrial Strategy.

54 Author's calculations, using data from Department for Transport road traffic estimates, table series TRA0106, various years. See 'Road Traffic Statistics (TRA)', Department for Transport, last modified 28 April 2021, https://www.gov.uk/government/statistical-data-sets/road-traffic-statistic s-tra (accessed 15 March 2022).

55 United Nations, *United Nations Framework Convention on Climate Change* (United Nations, 1992), 9, http://unfccc.int/files/essential_back ground/background_publications_htmlpdf/application/pdf/conveng.pdf (accessed 15 March 2022).

56 The severity of the detrimental health effects of air pollution became better understood thanks to work by the Committee on the Medical Effects of Air Pollutants, established in 1992, leading to the formation of national 'Air Quality Strategies' from 1997 onwards. See 'Air Quality in the UK', *Postnote* 188 (November 2002): 1–4, https://www.parliament.uk/globalass ets/documents/post/pn188.pdf (accessed 15 March 2022).

57 The latest pre-Covid-19, figures show that the railways receive £11.6 billion in fare income. See 'Rail Industry Finance (UK)', Office of Rail and Road. Bus industry revenue in Britain hovers between £6 and £7 billion a year, in real terms, pre-Covid-19, according to data from the Department for Transport, Table BUS0401a. See 'Costs, Fares and Revenue (BUS04)',

Department for Transport, https://www.gov.uk/government/statistical-data-sets/bus04-costs-fares-and-revenue (accessed 16 March 2022). The data does not differentiate the bus industry's fare income from the substantial amount of public subsidy received. Even if all of its income was counted as fare income, the combined rail and bus industries' fare income would remain comfortably short of the government's lost fuel duty income.

58 Philip Alston, Bassam Khawaja and Rebecca Riddell, *Public Transport, Private Profit: The Human Cost of Privatizing Buses in the United Kingdom* (Center for Human Rights and Global Justice, July 2021), 13, https://chrgj.org/wp-content/uploads/2021/07/Report-Public-Transport-Private-Profit.pdf (accessed 15 March 2022).

59 Sustrans, *Locked Out: Transport Poverty in England* (Sustrans, 2012), https://www.sustrans.org.uk/media/3706/transport-poverty-england-2012.pdf (accessed 15 March 2022).

60 Dave Prentis, 'How Tax Cuts for the Rich Have Cost the Country Dear', *New Statesman*, 18 November 2017, https://www.newstatesman.com/politics/uk-politics/2017/11/how-tax-cuts-rich-have-cost-country-dear (accessed 15 March 2022).

Chapter 3

1 'Northern Rail: Strikes Halted by "Breakthrough"', *BBC News*, 6 February 2019, https://www.bbc.co.uk/news/uk-england-manchester-47145551 (accessed 15 March 2022).

2 Helen Pidd, 'Northern Rail Plan to Remove Guards Faces Statutory Opposition', *Guardian*, 28 November 2018, https://www.theguardian.com/uk-news/2018/nov/28/northern-rail-plan-to-remove-train-guards-faces-statutory-opposition (accessed 15 March 2022).

3 Estimate by Professor Dave Cooper of the University of Chichester. See 'UK Economy Loses £300 Million since Start of Southern Trains Dispute', *The Argus*, 20 December 2016, https://www.theargus.co.uk/news/14976880.uk-economy-loses-300–million-since-start-of-southern-trains-dispute/ (accessed 15 March 2022).

4 James Arrowsmith, 'Post-Privatisation Industrial Relations in the UK Rail and Electricity Industries', *Industrial Relations Journal* 34, no. 2 (2003): 150–163, doi: 10.1111/1468-2338.00265.

5 Ibid. See also Foster, *Economics of Rail Privatisation*, for an account of how rail privatisation's structure was designed to reduce labour costs through inter-worker competition.

6   Author's calculation from figures presented in Office of Rail and Road statistics, Table 7226. See 'Welcome to the ORR Data Portal', Office of Rail and Road.

7   Calculated from figures presented in Robert Jupe and Gerald Crompton, "'A Deficient Performance": The Regulation of the Train Operating Companies in Britain's Privatised Railway System', *Critical Perspectives on Accounting* 17, no. 8 (2006): 1035–1065, doi: 10.1016/j.cpa.2005.10.002.

8   Ibid., 1052.

9   See, for example, Christian Wolmar, *Broken Rails: How Privatisation Wrecked Britain's Railways* (Aurum Press, 2001); Andrew Murray, *Off the Rails: The Crisis on Britain's Railways* (Verso, 2002).

10 See, for example, Rico Merkert, 'The Restructuring and Future of the British Rail System'. Institute for Transport Studies, University of Leeds. Working Paper 586, 2005, https://eprints.whiterose.ac.uk/2288/ (accessed 15 March 2022); John Hibbs et al., eds, *The Railways, the Market and the Government* (Institute of Economic Affairs, 2006).

11 Stephen Glaister and Tony Travers, *New Directions in British Railways? The Political Economy of Privatisation and Regulation* (Institute of Economic Affairs, 1993).

12 Stephen Glaister, *British Rail Privatisation: Competition Destroyed by Politics* (Centre for the Study of Regulated Industries, 2004), https://pdf4pro.com/cdn/british-rail-privatisation-university-of-bath-4a4380.pdf (accessed 15 March 2022).

13 Glaister, *British Rail Privatisation*, 53.

14 John Farrington and Richard McKenzie, 'Bus Deregulation in Scotland: A Preliminary View', *Scottish Geographical Magazine* 103, no. 1 (1987): 50–53, doi: 10.1080/00369228718736688; Christian Wolmar, *Stagecoach: A Classic Rags-to-Riches Tale from the Frontiers of Capitalism* (Orion, 1998).

15 P. M. Heseltine and D. T. Silcock, 'The Effects of Bus Deregulation on Costs', *Journal of Transport Economics and Policy* 24, no. 3 (1990): 239–254.

16 Glaister, *British Rail Privatisation*, 14–15.

17 Howard Botwinick, *Persistent Inequalities: Wage Disparity under Capitalist Competition* (Brill, 2017).

18 Glaister, *British Rail Privatisation*, 15.

19 Robert Jupe, 'A Model or a Policy Muddle? An Evaluation of Rail Franchising in the UK', *Public Money & Management* 30, no. 6 (2010): 347–354 (349), doi: 10.1080/09540962.2010.525002.

20 Campaign for Better Transport, *The Future of the Bus: Future Funding Arrangements* (Campaign for Better Transport, 2019), https://bettertransp

ort.org.uk/sites/default/files/research-files/future-bus-funding-arrangeme
nts.pdf (accessed 15 March 2022).

21 Data for 2021 in Figure 3.1 is provisional, with an update from the Office
of National Statistics expected shortly. All other data has been revised post
hoc by the Office for National Statistics. Figures are gross, inclusive of
overtime. Caution should be exercised when reading across the 'average'
category, given the changes in job categories employed by the Office for
National Statistics, with new categories replacing older ones in the early
2000s. However, it does give some overall indication of rail workers' wages
over time, according to the best available data. In particular, note that
in 1998 and 1999 only the data for 'rail engine drivers and assistants' are
reported, so the 'average' displayed here for those years does not account
for lower paid staff.

22 Foster, *Economics of Rail Privatisation*, 11.

23 *The Navigators*, directed by Ken Loach (Alta Films; Parallax Pictures;
Road Movies Filmproduktion; Tornasol Films; WDR/Arte, 2001).

24 'Too Close for Comfort', *The Construction Index*, 23 May 2019, https://ww
w.theconstructionindex.co.uk/news/view/too-close-for-comfort (accessed
15 March 2022).

25 Roy McNulty, *Realising the Potential of GB Rail: Final Independent Report
of the Rail Value for Money Study – Detailed Report* (Department for
Transport and Office of Rail Regulation, 2011), 207, https://assets.publ
ishing.service.gov.uk/government/uploads/system/uploads/attachment_d
ata/file/4204/realising-the-potential-of-gb-rail.pdf (accessed 15 March
2022).

26 Strangleman, *Work Identity*, 148.

27 As Wolmar notes, driver pay inflation was one of the great 'unintended
consequences' of privatisation. But he does not explain the point fully.
Wolmar, *On the Wrong Line*, chap. 3, n. 13.

28 Beverly Silver, *Forces of Labor: Workers' Movements and Globalization since
1870* (Cambridge University Press, 2003).

29 These subjective factors are sometimes referred to as 'associational power'
(as distinct from 'structural power'), e.g. in Erik Olin Wright, 'Working-
Class Power, Capitalist-Class Interests, and Class Compromise', *American
Journal of Sociology* 105, no. 4 (2000): 957–1002, doi: 10.1086/210397.

30 McNulty, *Realising the Potential of GB Rail*, 214.

31 Ibid., 208.

32 The exact amount of compensation paid by the government to train
operating companies for strikes is not publicly available. However, leaked

information reveals that the government paid £50 million in compensation to Govia Thameslink Railway. See Steven Swinford, 'Taxpayers Foot £50m bill for Southern Rail Strike Chaos as Ministers Prepare to Tighten Law', *Telegraph*, 14 December 2016, https://www.telegraph.co.uk/news/2016/12/13/taxpayers-foot-50million-bill-southern-rail-strike-chaos-ministers/. In a parliamentary question, it was revealed that South-West Trains had made application for financial compensation from the government with respect to losses incurred from the guards' strike. The then minister refused to reveal the extent of the compensation, citing 'commercial confidentiality'. The RMT claimed that it was of the order of £86 million – a deduction made by a study of published company accounts. See '£86 Million of Taxpayer's Money to South Western Railway', *RMT*, 29 November 2019, https://www.rmt.org.uk/news/86-million-of-taxpayers-money-to-south-western-railway/#:~:text=RMT%20Press%20Office%3A,is%20politically%20motivated%20says%20RMT. Finally, it was revealed that the Northern train operating company received a top-up subsidy of £22 million during the first year of the guards' strike on its franchise. While the information available publicly cannot 'prove' that these payments were compensation for money lost to strikes, they were significant payments over and above the subsidy Northern was due to receive, and the strikes were the most important factor in the company's greater than expected losses for that period. See 'New Arriva Rail North Accounts Reveal Secret Extra Payments', *RMT*, 3 January 2019, https://www.rmt.org.uk/news/new-arriva-rail-north-accounts3119/. Some franchise contracts carry zero 'revenue risk' – meaning that the government collects all fares paid to a train operating company in return for a flat management fee. This was the case with GTR. See National Audit Office, *The Thameslink, Southern and Great Northern Rail Franchise* (National Audit Office, 10 January 2018), 15–16, https://www.nao.org.uk/wp-content/uploads/2018/01/The-Thameslink-Southern-and-Great-Northern-rail-franchise.pdf (all websites accessed 15 March 2022). The exact scale of the huge losses of income that accrued to the government as a result of the Southern strike has not been made publicly available.

33 Chris Ames, 'Public in the Dark over Southern Dispute Fault Line', *Transport Network*, 27 October 2016, https://www.transport-network.co.uk/Public-in-the-dark-over-Southern-dispute-faul-tline/13432 (accessed 15 March 2022).

34 National Audit Office, *The Thameslink, Southern and Great Northern Rail Franchise*, 8.

35 Conrad Landin, 'Keeping Up with the Commuters: The Story of the Failure of Southern Rail', *New Statesman*, 14 December 2016, https://www. newstatesman.com/politics/uk/2016/12/keeping-commuters-story-failure-southern-rail (accessed 15 March 2022). The Westminster government's intransigence stood in stark contrast to the attitude of the Scottish government, which quickly resolved its dispute with the RMT over new trains in October 2016 by guaranteeing a guard on every ScotRail train: 'RMT Members Accept Scotrail Deal over Guards', *BBC News*, 5 October 2016, https://www.bbc.co.uk/news/uk-scotland-37560012 (accessed 15 March 2022).

36 'Rail Strikes are on this Week Causing Misery across the South', *Meridian*, 25 April 2016, https://www.itv.com/news/meridian/2016-04-25/rail-strik es-are-on-this-week-causing-misery-across-the-south (accessed 15 March 2022).

37 'Southern Rail Strike: 48-hour Walkout Causes Chaos for Commuters', *BBC News*, 13 December 2016, https://www.bbc.co.uk/news/uk-englan d-38296623 (accessed 15 March 2022).

38 Graeme Paton, 'Train Drivers Agree 28% Pay Rise to End Southern Rail Strikes', *The Times*, 9 November 2017, www.thetimes.co.uk/article/aslef-rail-union-ends-southern-dispute-with-14-000-pay-deal-xtxtljc87 (accessed 15 March 2022).

39 This is not to say that Southern drivers 'sold out' as such. In fact, they had already defied ASLEF leadership to vote against a previous deal, in a highly unusual move. Also, Govia Thameslink Railway had maintained a strategy of taking ASLEF to court to prevent strikes, which cost the union a great deal of money. In that circumstance ASLEF's leadership may have felt as though they had no option but to negotiate a deal, despite drivers' continued concerns about driver-only operation. This was certainly what the RMT's general secretary Mick Cash thought, although one has to take into account the need for trade union leaders to maintain a certain level of diplomacy with each other. See Paul Stephen, 'DOO Divides an Industry', *Rail* 862 (26 September–9 October 2018): 102–108.

40 Paul Stephen, 'DOO: Driving Efficiency or a Safety Risk?', *Rail*, 6 December 2019, https://www.railmagazine.com/news/rail-features/doo-driving-efficiency-or-a-safety-risk (accessed 15 March 2022).

41 The RMT has not published data on the combined effect of the strikes over various train operating companies, but this can be deduced from various media sources (all websites accessed 15 March 2022):

- Southern/GTR: 40 days (Simon Calder, 'Southern Rail Strike Update: Passengers Face 40th Day of Disruption as Britain's Longest-Running Industrial Dispute Continues', *Independent*, 12 March 2018, https:// www.independent.co.uk/travel/news-and-advice/southern-rail-strike-dates-latest-updates-today-trains-cancelled-delayed-a8251671.html).
- Greater Anglia: 8 days ('Dates Confirmed for Two Strikes by Greater Anglia Train Staff', *ITV News*, 19 September 2017, https://www.itv.com/ news/anglia/2017-09-19/dates-confirmed-for-two-strikes-by-greater-an glia-train-staff; 'Greater Anglia Workers Announce 48 Hour Strike', *ITV News*, 24 October 2017, www.itv.com/news/anglia/update/2017-10-24/greater-anglia-workers-announce-48-hour-strike/; 'New Dates on SWR and Greater Anglia Guards Dispute', *RMT*, 13 December 2017, https://www.rmt.org.uk/news/new-dates-on-swr-and-greater-anglia-guards-dispute/; 'Greater Anglia to Run Full Timetable During Planned RMT Strike in January', *Greater Anglia*, 5 January 2018, https://www.greateranglia.co.uk/about-us/news-desk/news-articles/gr eater-anglia-run-full-timetable-during-planned-rmt-strike-in).
- Merseyrail: 15 days ('RMT Members Vote for Action on Merseyrail', *RMT*, 28 February 2017; 'Northern, Southern Rail and Merseyrail Staff on Strike', *BBC News*, 14 March 2017, https://www.bbc.co.uk/news/ uk-england-39232062; 'Southern, Merseyrail and Arriva Trains North Strikes Announced', *BBC News*, 21 March 2017, https://www.bbc.co.uk/ news/uk-england-39339782; Liam Thorp, 'There will be Three Strikes on Merseyrail Next Month – Including during the Open', *Liverpool Echo*, 22 June 2017, https://www.liverpoolecho.co.uk/news/liverpool-news/ three-strikes-merseyrail-next-month-13224665; 'Northern, Southern and Merseyrail Strikes Set for September', *BBC News*, 18 August 2017, https://www.bbc.co.uk/news/uk-england-40975570; 'Northern, Merseyrail and Southern Rail Staff Strike', *BBC News*, 1 September 2017, https://www.bbc.co.uk/news/uk-england-41109806; 'Rail Strikes Continue to Hit Services across England', *BBC News*, 3 October 2017, https://www.bbc.co.uk/news/uk-england-41481821; 'Merseyrail Staff Announce Pre-Christmas Walkout over Guard Dispute', *BBC News*, 7 December 2017, https://www.bbc.co.uk/news/uk-england-merseyside-42271592; Alistair Houghton, 'Merseyrail Staff will Strike Three Times in a Week in January in Train Guards Row', *Liverpool Echo*, 20 December 2017, https://www.liverpoolecho.co.uk/news/ liverpool-news/merseyrail-staff-strike-three-times-14063299).

- ScotRail: 12 days ('RMT Confirms Campaign of Industrial Action on Scotrail over Driver Only Operation', *RMT*, 14 June 2016, https://www.rmt.org.uk/news/rmt-confirms-campaign-of-industrial-action-on-sco trail140616/; 'RMT Confirms Fresh Campaign of Industrial Action on Scotrail over Driver Only Operation', *RMT*, 30 June 2016, https://www.rmt.org.uk/news/rmt-confirms-fresh-campaign-of-indus trial-action-on-scotrail/; 'RMT Confirms New Dates in Campaign of Industrial Action on Scotrail over Driver Only Operation', *RMT*, 18 July 2016, https://www.rmt.org.uk/news/rmt-confirms-new-dates-of-industrial-action-on-scotrail/).
- Virgin Trains East Coast: 1 day ('Virgin Trains East Coast Strike "Solid" Says RMT', *BBC News*, 3 October 2016, https://www.bbc.co.uk/news/uk-37537264).
- South-West Trains: 27 days ('South Western Railway Guard Strikes Suspended', *BBC News*, 3 March 2020, https://www.bbc.co.uk/news/uk-england-51727642).
- Northern: 47 days ('Northern Rail: Halted by "Breakthrough"', *BBC News*).
- West Midlands Trains: 3 days ('Strike Action on West Midlands Trains Services Suspended', *BBC News*, 5 December 2019, https://www.bbc.co.uk/news/uk-england-50678548).

42 Stephen, 'DOO Divides an Industry'.

43 Mick Cash to Ian Prosser, 16 October 2017, https://www.rmt.org.uk/news/publications/letter-from-safety-regulator/letter-from-safety-regulat or-to-rmt.pdf (accessed 15 March 2022).

44 'Heroic RMT Guards Beat Back Northern Rail in Fight against Dangerous Driver-Only Operation', Socialist Party, 13 February 2019, https://www.soci alistparty.org.uk/articles/28673/13–02–2019/heroic-rmt-guards-beat-back-northern-rail-in-fight-against-dangerous-driver-only-operation (accessed 15 March 2022).

45 Vicky Gayle, 'Greater Anglia "Guarantees" Guards on Trains', *Gazette*, 19 July 2018, https://www.gazette-news.co.uk/news/16365477.greater-anglia-guarantees-guards-trains/ (accessed 15 March 2022).

46 'Merseyrail Strikes Called Off after New Agreement', *Railnews*, 17 October 2019, https://www.railnews.co.uk/news/2019/10/17-merseyrail-strikes-calle d-off-after.html (accessed 15 March 2022).

47 'RMT Members Accept Scotrail Deal over Guards', *BBC News*, 5 October 2016, https://www.bbc.co.uk/news/uk-scotland-37560012 (accessed 15 March 2022).

48 'Virgin East Coast Strike Called Off after "Progress" Talks', *BBC News*, 24 April 2017, https://www.bbc.co.uk/news/uk-england-39698139 (accessed 15 March 2022).

49 Tom Woodcock, 'West Midlands RMT Guards Jobs Saved', Socialist Party, 8 January 2020, https://m.socialistparty.org.uk/articles/30085/08-01-2020/west-midlands-rmt-guards-jobs-saved (accessed 15 March 2022). Some of these agreements are 'final', and some depend on further negotiation and relate to the imminent introduction of new rolling stock.

50 'South Western Railway Guard Strikes Suspended', *BBC News*.

51 Mick Cash, 'Fighting DOO', *RMT News*, November–December 2019, 3.

52 *Evening Standard*, 18 July 2002, cited in Gregor Gall, *Bob Crow: Socialist, Leader, Fighter: A Political Biography* (Manchester University Press, 2017), 182.

53 *Times*, 5 September 2007, cited in Gall, *Bob Crow*, 183.

54 *Telegraph*, 11 June 2009, cited in Gall, *Bob Crow*, 183.

55 Gall, *Bob Crow*, 183–184.

56 Christian Wolmar, 'Union and Management Should Grow Up', Christian Wolmar, 10 June 2009, https://www.christianwolmar.co.uk/2009/06/union-and-management-should-grow-up/ (accessed 15 March 2022).

57 Ralph Darlington, 'Leadership and Union Militancy: The Case of the RMT', *Capital & Class* 33, no. 3 (2009): 3–32, doi: 10.1177/030981680903300301011; Gall, *Bob Crow*.

58 Andrew Cumbers, Danny MacKinnon and Jon Shaw, 'Labour, Organisational Rescaling and the Politics of Production: Union Renewal in the Privatised Rail Industry', *Work, Employment and Society* 24, no. 1 (2010): 127–144, doi: 10.1177/0950017009353668.

59 Darlington, 'Leadership and Union Militancy'.

60 These figures are even worse since the Covid-19 crisis, at 12 per cent and 54 per cent respectively. See Disabled Persons Transport Advisory Committee, *Reductions in Assistance Capability at Stations*, The Association of British Commuters, 16 November 2020, https://abcommuters.com/2020/11/16/exclusive-accessibility-under-threat-due-to-increase-in-driver-only-trains-and-unstaffed-stations/ (accessed 15 March 2022).

61 Keith Richards to Nusrat Ghani and Andrew Jones, 9 April 2019, https://abcommuters.files.wordpress.com/2020/11/6b220-dptacs-letter-to-ministers-dated-9th-april-sent-2nd-may-2.pdf (accessed 15 March 2022).

62 See, for example, Govia Thameslink Railways' accessible travel policy: Thameslink, Southern and Great Northern, 'Accessible Travel Policy' (Thameslink, Southern and Great Northern, n.d.), https://www.south

ernrailway.com/-/media/goahead/gtr-all-shared-pdfs-and-documents/at
p-accessibility-documents/atp-policy.pdf?la=en (accessed 15 March 2022).

63 Ann Frye Limited, Rail Accessibility Ltd and MWW Transport
    Consultants, *On Track for 2020? The Future of Accessible Rail Travel: Final
    Report* (Association of Train Operating Companies, 2015), 30–32, https://
    www.railhub2.co.uk/rh6/archive/docs/2017-06-30%20RDG%20On%20
    track%20for%202020.pdf (accessed 15 March 2022).

64 RMT, *The Role of the Guard: What Our Members Say* (RMT, 4 October
    2018), https://www.rmt.org.uk/news/public-document-library/the-role-
    of-the-guard-what-our-members-say/ (accessed 15 March 2022).

65 Stephanie Tobyn, *Condition 5 of the Passenger and Station Licences –
    Disabled People's Protection Policy (DPPP) – Letter* (Office of Rail and
    Road, 10 November 2017), https://www.orr.gov.uk/media/10603/down-
    load (accessed 15 March 2022).

66 'Disability Festival Organisers Left Stranded by Southern', *Sussex World*, 8
    November 2017, https://www.sussexexpress.co.uk/news/disability-festival-
    organisers-left-stranded-by-southern-1070914 (accessed 15 March 2022).

67 Arriva Rail North Limited, annual report and financial statements for the
    year ending 31 March 2019.

68 Gourvish, *British Rail 1974–97*, 46.

69 See, for example, the Association of British Commuters ('ABC: Association
    of British Commuters', Association of British Commuters, https://abcom
    muters.com/ (accessed 17 March 2022)); Disabled People Against Cuts
    ('Please Respond to Vital Consultation on Driver Only Operated Trains –
    by January 31st', Disabled People Against Cuts, 23 January 2018, https://
    dpac.uk.net/2018/01/please-respond-to-vital-consultation-on-driver-only-
    operated-trains-by-january-31st/ (accessed 15 March 2022)); the National
    Pensioners Convention (Sharon Sukhram, 'Passengers Want a Properly
    Staffed Railway, Not More Driver-Only-Operated Trains', *Touch Stone*,
    20 June 2016, https://touchstoneblog.org.uk/2016/06/passengers-want-
    properly-staffed-railway-not-driver-operated-trains/ (accessed 15 March
    2022)); and the work of activists such as Ann Bates (John Pring, 'Ministers'
    Plans on "Toxic" Impact of Driver-Only Trains Fall Way Short, Says
    DPTAC', *Disability News Service*, 1 August 2019, https://www.disabili
    tynewsservice.com/ministers-plans-on-toxic-impact-of-driver-only-trains-
    fall-way-short-says-dptac/ (accessed 15 March 2022)) and Doug
    Paulley (Doug Paulley, 'Driver Controlled Operation and Staffing
    of Stations', https://www.kingqueen.org.uk/doo/ (accessed 17 March
    2022)).

70 RMT, *Role of the Guard*; Paul Stephen, 'Is There a Way to Break the DOO Stalemate?', *Rail*, 9 December 2018, https://www.railmagazine.com/ news/rail-features/is-there-a-way-to-break-the-doo-stalemate (accessed 15 March 2022).

71 Richard Locke and Lucio Baccaro, 'The Resurgence of Italian Unions?' *Perspectives on Work* 3, no. 1 (1999): 18–22; Mike Rigby and Mari Luz Marco Aledo, 'The Worst Record in Europe? A Comparative Analysis of Industrial Conflict in Spain', *European Journal of Industrial Relations* 7, no. 3 (2001): 287–305, doi: 10.1177/095968010173004; Heather Connolly and Ralph Darlington, 'Radical Political Unionism in France and Britain: A Comparative Study of SUD-Rail and the RMT', *European Journal of Industrial Relations* 18, no. 3 (2012): 235–250, doi: 10.1177/0959680112452693; Matthias Beestermöller, 'Striking Evidence? Demand Persistence for Inter-City Buses from German Railway Strikes', Discussion Papers in Economics 31768, University of Munich, Department of Economics, 2017, https://ideas.repec.org/p/lmu/muenec/31768.html (accessed 15 March 2022).

Chapter 4

1 Anon., cited in Shaw, *Competition, Regulation and the Privatisation of British Rail*, 112–113.

2 Bowman et al., *The Great Train Robbery*, 43.

3 These have been named 'performance bonds'. For more details see National Audit Office, *The InterCity East Coast Passenger Rail Franchise* (National Audit Office, 24 March 2011), https://www.nao.org.uk/wp-content/uploads/2011/03/1011824.pdf (accessed 15 March 2022).

4 For some critical commentary, see House of Commons Committee of Public Accounts, *Reform of the Rail Franchising Programme* (Stationery Office, 12 February 2016), https://publications.parliament.uk/pa/ cm201516/cmselect/cmpubacc/600/600.pdf (accessed 15 March 2022). Before the Covid-19 outbreak, the government was struggling to attract more than two bidders for franchises, much fewer than the number considered in the industry to be competitive. See *Rail Franchising: Ninth Report of Session 2016–17* (Stationery Office, 30 January 2017, https://publica tions.parliament.uk/pa/cm201617/cmselect/cmtrans/66/66.pdf (accessed 15 March 2022).

5 In this section, I am indebted to arguments first made by Bowman et al., *The Great Train Robbery*.

6 Roy McNulty, *Rail Value for Money: Scoping Study Report* (Department for Transport, 31 March 2010), https://www.railwaysarchive.co.uk/docu ments/McNulty_RailVFMScoping2010.pdf (accessed 15 March 2022).

7 Bowman et al., *The Great Train Robbery*, 140.

8 Cited in ibid., 142.

9 McNulty, *Realising the Potential of GB Rail*, 285.

10 Ofwat, *Financial Performance and Expenditure of the Water Companies in England and Wales 2009–10* (Ofwat, n.d.), https://web.archive.org/ web/20121031184820/http://www.ofwat.gov.uk/regulating/reporting/rpt_f pe_2009-10.pdf. McNulty also goes on to cite a consultants' report commissioned for his study. That report, written by the LEK consultancy, refers to European data on total factor productivity, which is at such a high level of abstraction across so many different industries in different countries as to be irrelevant to discussing rail ownership, and data from Ofwat, which is merely a snapshot of 'efficiency' in a given year, with no definition given for what efficiency means in that context. See LEK, *Alternative Railway Structures: Final Report*, vol. 1 (LEK Consulting, 7 March 2011), 75–76. In fact, any rounded view of water in Britain would need to contend with the fact that tens of thousands of jobs were lost from the industry after privatisation, that the sector has been racked by the scandal of burst waterpipes and the contamination of rivers and seas by sewerage, that capital spending has fallen as bills have increased and that it is taking on ever greater quantities of debt to fund shareholder dividend payments, which threaten to require huge public bailouts sooner or later. See Kate Bayliss and David Hall, *Bringing Water into Public Ownership: Costs and Benefits* (Public Services International Research Unit, May 2017), https://gala.gre.ac.uk/id/eprint/17277/10/17277%20HALL_ Bringing_Water_into_Public_Ownership_%28Rev%27d%29_2017.pdf; Karol Yearwood, *The Privatised Water Industry in the UK: An ATM for Investors* (Public Services International Research Unit, September 2018); David Hall, *Water and Sewerage Company Finances 2021: Dividends and Investment – and Company Attempts to Hide Dividends* (Public Services International Research Unit, 28 January 2022), https://gala.gre.ac.uk/ id/eprint/34274/14/34274%20HALL_Water_and_Sewerage_Company_ Finances_%28Rev.2%29_2021.pdf (all websites accessed 15 March 2022).

11 McNulty, *Realising the Potential of GB Rail*, 285.

12 Andrew Smith, Chris Nash and Phill Wheat, 'Passenger Rail Franchising in Britain: Has it been a Success?', *International Journal of Transport Economics* 36, no 1 (2009): 33–62 (54–55, 59). This is an updated version of an original

conference paper by Andrew Smith and Phill Wheat, which is the publication cited by McNulty. McNulty also cites a study on costs for public–private infrastructure projects on the London Underground after renationalisation. But the study is far more equivocal on observed rising costs after renationalisation than McNulty implies, and it says nothing about the costs of finance. See Office of the PPP Arbiter, *Final Benchmarking Reports* (14 October 2010), https://webarchive.nationalarchives.gov.uk/ukgwa/20110218141103mp_/ http://www.ppparbiter.org.uk/files/uploads/d_benchmarking/2010102210 4118_115678rkh%20Benchmarking%20Anonymised%20v01.pdf (accessed 15 March 2022). The big scandal of the London Underground's public–private partnerships was the significant rewards to shareholders and bondholders, despite contractual collapse and government bailout. See Robert Jupe, 'The Modernisation and Fragmentation of the UK's Transport Infrastructure', *Financial Accountability & Management* 27, no. 1 (2011): 43–62, doi: 10.1111/j.1468–0408.2010.00515.x.

13 Bowman et al., *The Great Train Robbery*, 142.
14 McNulty, *Realising the Potential of GB Rail*.
15 'High Noon at Marsham Street', *RailStaff*, 9 October 2012, www.rail staff.co.uk/2012/10/09/high-noon-at-marsham-street/ (accessed 15 March 2022); Richard Brown, interview by Chris Kinchin-Smith, Science Museum Group Collection, 3 July 2019, https://collection.sciencemuseu mgroup.org.uk/objects/co8728968/richard-brown-interviewed-by-chris-k inchin-smith-oral-history-interview (accessed 15 March 2022).
16 Patrick McLoughlin to Richard Brown, 15 October 2012, https://assets. publishing.service.gov.uk/government/uploads/system/uploads/attachme nt_data/file/9197/letter-to-richard-brown.pdf (accessed 15 March 2022).
17 Bowman et al., *The Great Train Robbery*.
18 'CTL Distinguished Speakers Series – Nicola Shaw', Massachusetts Institute of Technology Center for Transportation & Logistics, 26 February 2010, https://ctl.mit.edu/events/fri-02262010-0730/ctl-distin guished-speakers-series-nicola-shaw; 'Executive at Owner of Southern Railway Quits to Take Charge of HS1', *Belfast Telegraph*, 26 September 2016, https://www.belfasttelegraph.co.uk/business/news/executive-at-owne r-of-southern-railway-quits-to-take-charge-of-hs1-35078921.html (accessed 15 March 2022).
19 Chris Grayling, 'The Public has Lost Faith in the Railways after the Timetabling Chaos – It's Time for Change', *Telegraph*, 19 September 2018, www.telegraph.co.uk/business/2018/09/19/public-has-lost-faith-rail ways-timetabling-chaos-time-change/ (accessed 15 March 2022).

20 'Williams Rail Review', HM Government, https://www.gov.uk/govern ment/groups/rail-review (accessed 18 March 2022).

21 Grayling, 'The Public has Lost Faith'.

22 'Group Board', Royal Mail Group, https://www.royalmailgroup.com/en/ about-us/management-and-committees/royal-mail-group-board/ (accessed 18 March 2022).

23 'Williams Railways Review to Look at "All Options"', 7 December 2018, https://www.bbc.co.uk/news/business-46476431 (accessed 15 March 2022).

24 'Transparency Now: No More Secret Talks about the Future of our Railway', Association of British Commuters, 22 May https://abcommut ers.com/2020/05/22/transparency-now-no-more-secret-talks-about-the-fu ture-of-our-railway/ (accessed 15 March 2022).

25 Christian Wolmar, 'Creating the Passenger Rail Franchises', in *All Change: British Railway Privatisation*, edited by Roger Freeman and Jon Shaw (McGraw-Hill, 2000), 119–146 (140).

26 Andrew Haylen, *Rail Passenger Rights, Compensation & Complaints* (House of Commons Library, 20 May 2019), https://researchbriefings.files.parlia ment.uk/documents/CBP-8572/CBP-8572.pdf (accessed 15 March 2022).

27 See, for example, Amelia Wade, 'One in Five GTR and Northern Trains at Least 10 Minutes Late Following Timetable Chaos', Which?, 3 July 2018, https://www.which.co.uk/news/2018/07/one-in-five-gtr-and-northern-trains-were-late/ (accessed 15 March 2022); Ruth Mosalski, 'The Staggering Number of Transport for Wales Trains which are Cancelled or Delayed', *Wales Online*, 19 October 2021, https://www.walesonline.co.uk/news/ wales-news/staggering-number-transport-wales-trains-21888150 (accessed 15 March 2022); Jane Haynes, '"Worst Service in Years" – Commuter Fury over Cancelled Trains in and out of Birmingham', 4 November 2021, https://www.birminghammail.co.uk/news/midlands-news/worst-service-years-commuter-fury-22064551 (accessed 15 March 2022).

28 Department for Transport, *Rail Delays and Compensation 2020: Moving Britain Ahead* (Department for Transport, October 2020), https://assets.publishing.service.gov.uk/government/uploads/system/up loads/attachment_data/file/927876/rail-delays-and-compensation-report-2020.pdf (accessed 15 March 2022).

29 Oliver McKean, 'Revealed: How Train Companies are Adding Unnecessary Hassle to Claiming Compensation', Which?, 9 May 2019, https://www. which.co.uk/news/2019/05/revealed-how-train-companies-are-adding-unn ecessary-hassle-to-claiming-compensation/ (accessed 15 March 2022).

30 Department for Transport, *Rail Delays*.
31 This is not to say that there are not battles over levels of compensation paid by Network Rail to train operating companies, but train operating companies have staff whose job it is to get as much compensation as possible, whereas passengers are left to manage with their own resources.
32 In real terms (adjusted for inflation to 2020/21). Data from Network Rail Limited's regulated accounts, various years, and from the Department for Transport: see 'Train Operating Companies: Passenger's Charter Compensation', Department for Transport, 28 September 2021, https:// www.gov.uk/government/publications/train-operating-companies-passe ngers-charter-compensation#history (accessed 15 March 2022). Inflation data taken from Treasury inflation deflators. Since the Covid-19 outbreak, trends have reversed, and Network Rail has pocketed £347 million in payments *from* train operating companies for better-than-expected performance. However, this is based on very light utilisation of the network, which makes punctuality much easier to achieve, and these payments have been mostly funded by central government bailouts.
33 This issue, and campaigning around it in the House of Commons, are covered in Haylen, *Rail Passenger Rights*.
34 Ibid., 19.
35 'Getting a Good Deal for Transport Users', https://www.transportfocus. org.uk/ (accessed 18 March 2022).
36 Department for Transport, *Tailored Review: Transport Focus* (Department for Transport, July 2020, https://assets.publishing.service.gov.uk/gov ernment/uploads/system/uploads/attachment_data/file/927161/tailored-re view-tf.pdf (accessed 15 March 2022).
37 Wolmar, *On the Wrong Line*, chap. 2.
38 Spencer Stokes, 'Settle–Carlisle Line Thriving 30 Years On after Closure Threat', *BBC News*, 15 December 2013, https://www.bbc.co.uk/news/uk-england-leeds-25364686 (accessed 15 March 2022).
39 Foster, *Economics of Rail Privatisation*, 3.
40 Christian Wolmar, 'Settle – Carlisle Line was Turning Point in Rail History', *Rail*, 4 April 2014, https://www.christianwolmar.co.uk/2014/04/ rail-746-settle-carlisle-line-was-turning-point-in-rail-history (accessed 15 March 2022).
41 In the language of political theorist Antonio Gramsci, opposing railway line closures is 'common sense'. Achieving a change in common sense is vital for establishing stable political hegemony. See Antonio Gramsci, *Selections from the Prison Notebooks* (Lawrence and Wishart, 1971).

42 West Lindsey District Council, *State of the District Report* (West Lindsey District Council, 2020), https://www.west-lindsey.gov.uk/_resources/assets/attachment/full/0/114077.pdf (accessed 15 March 2022).

43 See 'Neglected Stations beyond the Fringe', *Rail*, 24 June 2015, https://www.railmagazine.com/infrastructure/stations/neglected-stations-beyond-the-fringe?p=3 (accessed 15 March 2022). It surely has not helped that the vast majority of services that call at Gainsborough Lea Road are Northern, not East Midlands Trains (now East Midlands Railway) services, giving the latter little incentive to improve station facilities.

44 See Friends of the Brigg & Lincoln Lines Gainsborough Rail and Bus Users Group, *Travel the Brigg Line* (Friends of the Brigg & Lincoln Lines Gainsborough Rail and Bus Users Group, n.d.), https://bettertransport.org.uk/sites/default/files/15.09.10.blg1.pdf (accessed 18 March 2022); 'Home', Friends of the Brigg & Lincoln Lines, https://web.archive.org/web/20150419011932/http://e-voice.org.uk/friendsofbrigg-lincolnlines/ (accessed 18 March 2022).

45 'Neglected Stations', *Rail*.

46 Ibid.

47 Since Covid-19 hit, the weekday service has been reduced to two runs each day, and there is seemingly little prospect of full service restoration, in the context of apparently permanent cuts to Northern's overall service levels, which have been mandated by central government. This is a stark example of how the fight for socially-necessary services is seldom ever 'won', but is a constant battle with government and rail industry over resourcing.

48 Graeme Pickering, 'Improving Rail Links in Lincolnshire', *Rail* 885 (14–27 August 2019): 42–47.

49 Transport Regeneration, *The Value of Community Rail Partnerships and the Value of Community Rail Volunteering* (National Community Rail Development Implementation Steering Group, January 2015), https://communityrail.org.uk/wp-content/uploads/2018/06/ACoRP-Value-of-CRPs-and-Volunteering-28.1.15.pdf (accessed 15 March 2022).

50 'Lords Slam "Poor Rail Services"', *BBC News*, 15 January 2007, http://news.bbc.co.uk/1/hi/england/wiltshire/6264911.stm (accessed 15 March 2022).

51 'Passengers in Rush-Hour Protest', *BBC News*, 22 January 2007, http://news.bbc.co.uk/1/hi/england/6285629.stm (accessed 15 March 2022).

52 Despite First Great Western's warnings, there are no records of prosecutions related to the fare strike. Indeed, the manager of Bristol Temple Meads claimed that there would be no prosecutions, while at Bath Spa,

forty passengers are reported as having been let through gates using the fake tickets. See 'Confusion over Fake Rail Tickets', *BBC News*, 28 January 2008, http://news.bbc.co.uk/1/hi/england/7212697.stm (accessed 15 March 2022); Haroon Siddique and Agencies, 'Angry Commuters Hold Rail Fares "Strike"', *Guardian*, 28 January 2008.

53 'Confusion over Fake Rail Tickets', *BBC News*.

54 'Train Operator Sorry for Service', *BBC News*, 22 January 2008, http://news.bbc.co.uk/1/hi/england/7202336.stm (accessed 15 March 2022).

55 Dave Gibson, 'Freedom Riders Force Talks from Rail Bosses', *Socialist Worker*, 19 August 2014, https://socialistworker.co.uk/news/freedom-rid ers-force-talks-from-rail-bosses (accessed 15 March 2022).

56 South Yorkshire Freedom Riders, *Who We Are and Where We Started* (Future Years, n.d.), www.futureyears.org.uk/uploads/files/South%20 Yorkshire%20Freedom%20Riders%20the%20story%20so%20far.pdf (accessed 25 March 2022).

57 The group's name, Freedom Riders, was borrowed from a movement in the United States in the early 1960s to end racial segregation on buses. See Raymond Arsenault, *Freedom Riders: 1961 and the Struggle for Racial Justice* (Oxford University Press, 2011).

58 John Grayson, 'Barnsley Freedom Riders: Pensioner People Power', *Open Democracy*, 9 May 2014, https://www.opendemocracy.net/en/shine-a-lig ht/barnsley-freedom-riders-pensioner-people-power/ (accessed 15 March 2022); South Yorkshire Freedom Riders, *Who We Are*.

59 Tony Nuttall, 'No Ticket to Ride: An Arrested Freedom Rider Writes', *Guardian*, 4 July 2014, https://www.theguardian.com/uk-news/the-north erner/2014/jul/04/arrested-freedom-rider-tony-nuttall-writes (accessed 15 March 2022); George Torr, 'South Yorkshire's Freedom Riders: What Happened and When', *The Star*, 6 August 2020, https://www.thestar. co.uk/news/politics/council/south-yorkshires-freedom-riders-what-happe ned-and-when-2935209 (accessed 15 March 2022).

60 Nuttall, 'No Ticket to Ride'.

61 Dave Gibson, 'Charges against Barnsley Freedom Riders Dropped', *Socialist Worker*, 28 November 2014, https://socialistworker.co.uk/news/ charges-against-barnsley-freedom-riders-dropped/ (accessed 15 March 2022).

62 Torr, 'South Yorkshire's Freedom Riders'; South Yorkshire Freedom Riders, *Who We Are*.

63 Urban Transport Group, *Bus Policy* (Urban Transport Group, November 2020), https://www.urbantransportgroup.org/system/files/general-docs/

Bus%20Policy%20Version%202020%20%281%29.pdf (accessed 15 March 2022).

64 Alston, Khawaja and Riddell, *Public Transport, Private Profit*, 6.

65 Ashlie Blakey, 'Greater Manchester to Get £1 Billion Transport Boost in Government "Levelling-Up" Package', *Manchester Evening News*, 23 October 2021, https://www.manchestereveningnews.co.uk/news/greater-manchester-news/greater-manchester-1-billion-transport-21948065 (accessed 15 March 2022).

66 See 'Get Glasgow Moving', https://www.getglasgowmoving.org/news/ (accessed 19 March 2022).

67 See examples from Chicago and Michigan: 'Chicago Public Transit Fare Strike Called', *UPI*, 9 December 2004, https://www.upi.com/Business_News/2004/12/09/Chicago-public-transit-fare-strike-called/43501102609477/ (accessed 15 March 2022); '"Michigan is on Fire": Historic Fare Strike Hits Buses in Grand Rapids, MI', ATU, https://www.atu.org/media/releases/michigan-is-on-fire-historic-fare-strike-hits-buses-in-grand-rapids-mi (accessed 23 October 2021). Fare strikes in Santiago de Chile escalated into a more general movement for social reform and wealth redistribution, culminating recently in the election of leftist and former student leader Gabriel Boric: John Bartlett, 'Chile Students' Mass Fare-Dodging Expands into City-Wide Protest', *Guardian*, 18 October 2019, https://www.theguardian.com/world/2019/oct/18/chile-students-mass-fare-dodging-expands-into-city-wide-protest (accessed 15 March 2022); Gladys Piérola, 'Un año después: la frenética y tensa negociación del acuerdo constitucional en tres momentos', *Pauta*, 15 November 2020, https://www.pauta.cl/politica/tres-momentos-de-la-negociacion-acuerdo-constitucional-15-de-noviembre (accessed 15 March 2022).

68 National Rail, *National Rail Conditions of Travel: From 6th February 2022* (National Rail, n.d.), 7, https://www.nationalrail.co.uk/National%20Rail%20Conditions%20of%20Travel.pdf (accessed 15 March 2022).

69 Calculated from the latest pre-Covid statistics with data from Department for Transport statistics, Table TSGB0102. See 'Modal Comparisons (TSGB01)', Department for Transport, 16 December 2021, https://www.gov.uk/government/statistical-data-sets/tsgb01-modal-comparisons (accessed 15 March 2022).

70 'Is Rail Nationalisation a Vote-Winner?', YouGov, 21 September 2015, https://yougov.co.uk/topics/politics/articles-reports/2015/09/21/is-rail-nationalisation-vote-winner; 'Do the Public Want the Railways

Renationalised?', Full Fact, 14 June 2018, https://fullfact.org/economy/do-public-want-railways-renationalised/ (accessed 15 March 2022).

Chapter 5

1   Department for Transport, *Great British Railways: The Williams–Shapps Plan for Rail* (Department for Transport, May 2021), https://assets.pub lishing.service.gov.uk/government/uploads/system/uploads/attachment_data/file/994603/gbr-williams-shapps-plan-for-rail.pdf (accessed 15 March 2022).

2   At the time of writing both of the major franchises in Scotland and Wales are run by publicly owned companies, although outsourcing and private ownership still persist in much of the rail systems in those nations, and services are also provided by private companies based in England. It is currently unknown what the Great British Rail proposals would mean for the devolved nations' renewed appetite for public ownership.

3   It is unclear whether they will ever be published.

4   Data from Office of Rail and Road statistics, Table 7270. See 'Welcome to the ORR Data Portal', Office of Rail and Road.

5   Gwyn Topham, '"Back to the Dad Old Days": Swingeing Rail Cuts Set Alarm Bells Ringing', *Guardian*, 5 December 2021, https://www.the guardian.com/business/2021/dec/05/back-bad-old-days-swingeing-rail-cu ts-alarm-bells-ringing (accessed 15 March 2022); Nicholas Hellen and Tom Calver, 'Rail Cuts Stay as £16bn Subsidies Withdrawn', *The Times*, 30 January 2022, www.thetimes.co.uk/article/rail-cuts-stay-as-16bn-subsi dies-withdrawn-7q5k5nd67 (accessed 15 March 2022).

6   Shaoul, 'Railpolitik'.

7   Intergovernmental Panel on Climate Change, *Climate Change 2022: Impacts, Adaptation and Vulnerability: Summary for Policymakers* (Intergovernmental Panel on Climate Change, 27 February 2022), https://report.ipcc.ch/ar6wg2/pdf/IPCC_AR6_WGII_FinalDraft_FullReport.p df (accessed 15 March 2022).

8   Suzanne Jeffery, 'Why We Need to Act – The Urgency of Now', in *Climate Jobs: Building a Workforce for the Climate Emergency*, edited by Suzanne Jeffery, 3–10 (4), Campaign Against Climate Change, 2021, https://www.cacctu.org.uk/sites/data/files/sites/data/files/Docs/climatejobs-2021-web.p df (accessed 15 March 2022).

9   The 'other' category in Figure 5.1 amalgamates the 'public', 'industrial processes' and 'land use, land use change and forestry' sectors.

10 An early study in travel patterns suggests that the proportion of people working from home increased from 4 per cent to 38 per cent during the early stages of the Covid-19 pandemic, although it is likely to have decreased since then as many employers have encouraged a return to work. See Greg Marsden, Jillian Anable, Iain Docherty and Llinos Brown, *At a Crossroads: Travel Adaptations during Covid-19 Restrictions and Where Next* (Centre for Research in Energy Demand Solutions and DecarboN8, March 2021), https://www.creds.ac.uk/wp-content/uploads/CREDS-De carbon8-covid-transas-briefing.pdf (accessed 15 March 2022). Also note that official figures do not count international aviation emissions, which account for 93 per cent of total emissions from flying and have increased by 138 per cent between 1990 and 2019, despite the fact that they are to be included in future carbon budgets. https://researchbriefings.files. parliament.uk/documents/CBP-8826/CBP-8826.pdf See David Hirst, *Aviation, Decarbonisation and Climate Change* (House of Commons Library, 20 September 2021), https://researchbriefings.files.parliament. uk/documents/CBP-8826/CBP-8826.pdf (accessed 15 March 2022); and 'Transport Statistics Great Britain: 2021', Department for Transport, 16 December 2021, https://www.gov.uk/government/statistics/transport-sta tistics-great-britain-2021/transport-statistics-great-britain-2021 (accessed 15 March 2022).

11 In Figure 5.2 the author's calculation amalgamates the domestic and international shipping and aviation categories, and excludes the smallest and least used emitters, such as motorcycles and 'other road transport emissions', which include, for example, the emissions from the evaporation of engine lubricants.

12 Greg Marsden et al., 'Decarbonising Transport: Getting Carbon Ambition Right', Centre for Research in Energy Demand Solutions, 5 September 2020, https://www.creds.ac.uk/publications/decarbonising-transport-gett ing-carbon-ambition-right/ (accessed 15 March 2022); Tahir Latif, 'Creating a Green, Affordable and Accessible Network for All: Climate Jobs in Transport', in *Climate Jobs: Building a Workforce for the Climate Emergency*, edited by Suzanne Jeffery, 49–66, Campaign Against Climate Change, 2021, https://www.cacctu.org.uk/sites/data/files/sites/data/files/ Docs/climatejobs-2021-web.pdf (accessed 15 March 2022).

13 'Transport Statistics Great Britain: 2021', Department for Transport.

14 Gareth Dale and Josh Moos, 'Jet Zero: A One Way Ticket to Climate Hell', *Ecologist*, 31 August 2021, https://theecologist.org/2021/aug/31/ jet-zero-one-way-ticket-climate-hell (accessed 15 March 2022).

15   Joseph Rowntree Foundation, *UK Poverty 2020/2021* (Joseph Rowntree Foundation, 2021), https://www.jrf.org.uk/file/57306/download?token=ir u3hRZo&filetype=full-report (accessed 15 March 2022).

16   Karen Lucas, Giulio Mattioli, Ersilia Verlinghieri and Alvaro Guzman, 'Transport Poverty and its Adverse Social Consequences', *Proceedings of the Institution of Civil Engineers – Transport* 169, no. 6 (2016): 353–365, doi: 10.1680/jtran.15.00073.

17   Karen Lucas, Tim Grosvenor and Roona Simpson, *Transport, the Environment and Social Exclusion* (Joseph Rowntree Foundation, 2021), https://citeseerx.ist.psu.edu/viewdoc/download?doi=10.1.1.474.1977&rep =rep1&type=pdf (accessed 15 March 2022).

18   Shivonne Gates et al., *Transport and Inequality: An Evidence Review for the Department for Transport* (NatCen, 10 July 2019), https://assets.publis hing.service.gov.uk/government/uploads/system/uploads/attachment_da ta/file/953951/Transport_and_inequality_report_document.pdf (accessed 15 March 2022).

19   Karen Lucas, Gordon Stokes, Jeroen Bastiaanssen and Julian Burkinshaw, *Inequalities in Mobility and Access in the UK Transport System* (Foresight and Government Office for Science, March 2019), https://assets.publish ing.service.gov.uk/government/uploads/system/uploads/attachment_data /file/784685/future_of_mobility_access.pdf (accessed 15 March 2022).

20   Lucas et al., *Inequalities in Mobility*, 6.

21   Office for National Statistics Table A47, various years. See 'Percentage of Households with Cars by Income Group, Tenure and Household Composition: Table A47', Office for National Statistics, 24 January 2019, https://www.ons.gov.uk/peoplepopulationandcommunity/personalandh ouseholdfinances/expenditure/datasets/percentageofhouseholdswithcarsb yincomegrouptenureandhouseholdcompositionuktablea47 (accessed 15 March 2022).

22   Giulio Mattioli, '"Forced Car Ownership" in the UK and Germany: Socio-Spatial Patterns and Potential Economic Stress Impacts', *Social Inclusion* 5, no. 4 (2017): 147–160, doi: 10.17645/si.v5i4.1081.

23   Angela Curl, Julie Clark and Ade Kearns, 'Household Car Adoption and Financial Distress in Deprived Urban Communities: A Case of Forced Car Ownership?', *Transport Policy* 65 (2018): 61–71, doi: 10.1016/j. tranpol.2017.01.002.

24   Barker and Connelly, cited in Lucas et al., *Inequalities in Mobility*, 17.

25   RAC Foundation, *The Cost of Transport and its Impact on UK Households: An Analysis of the ONS (2007) Family Spending Report* (RAC Foundation,

2009), https://www.racfoundation.org/assets/rac_foundation/content/do wnloadables/cost%20of%20transport%20-%20dainton%20-%20110308%2 0-%20report.pdf (accessed 15 March 2022).

26   Andrew Hood, Robert Joyce and David Sturrock, *Problem Debt and Low-Income Households* (Institute for Fiscal Studies, January 2018), https:// ifs.org.uk/uploads/publications/comms/R138%20-%20Problem%20debt. pdf (accessed 15 March 2022); Matthew Whittaker, *An Unhealthy Interest? Debt Distress and the Consequences of Raising Rates* (Resolution Foundation, February 2018), https://www.resolutionfoundation.org/ app/uploads/2018/02/Household-debt.pdf (accessed 15 March 2022).

27   Andy Burnham, Greater Manchester Combined Authority and Transport for Greater Manchester, *Change a Region to Change a Nation: Greater Manchester's Walking and Cycling Investment Plan* (Andy Burnham, Greater Manchester Combined Authority and Transport for Greater Manchester, 27 January 2020), 32, https://news.tfgm.com/resources/ change-a-region-to-change-a-nation-gm-cycling-and-walking-investmen t-plan-2020 (accessed 15 March 2022).

28   Jennifer Mindell and Saffron Karlsen, 'Community Severance and Health: What Do We Actually Know?', *Journal of Urban Health* 89, no. 2 (2012): 232–246 (235), doi: 10.1007/s11524-011-9637-7.

29   Joanna Barnes, Tim Chatterton and James Longhurst, 'Emissions vs Exposure: Increasing Injustice from Road Traffic-Related Air Pollution in the United Kingdom', *Transportation Research Part D: Transport and Environment* 73 (2019): 56–66, doi: 10.1016/j.trd.2019.05.012.

30   Tom Haines-Doran et al., 'Rethinking Value for Place-Based Economic Recovery: A "System-of-Systems" Approach to Housing Retrofit and "Green Book" Reform', unpublished paper, Yorkshire Universities, 2020.

31   Darren McCauley and Raphael Heffron, 'Just Transition: Integrating Climate, Energy and Environmental Justice', *Energy Policy* 119 (2018): 1–7, doi: 10.1016/j.enpol.2018.04.014.

32   As the Campaign Against Climate Change Trade Union Group has argued. See Latif, 'Creating a Green, Affordable and Accessible Network'.

33   Giulio Mattioli, Cameron Roberts, Julia Steinberger and Andrew Brown, 'The Political Economy of Car Dependence: A Systems of Provision Approach', *Energy Research & Social Science* 66 (2020), doi: 10.1016/j. erss.2020.101486.

34   Jeffery, 'Why We Need to Act', 5–6.

35   Author's calculation based on Department for Transport statistics, Table NTS0409b. See 'Modal Comparisons (TSGB01)', Department for

Transport. Equivalent data is not available for Scotland or Wales, to the best of the author's knowledge.

36   'Hybrid Working: Now for the Reality', Chartered Management Institute, 19 May 2021, https://www.managers.org.uk/knowledge-and-insights/arti cle/hybrid-working-now-for-the-reality/ (accessed 15 March 2022).

37   According to calculation by *The Independent*. See Simon Calder, 'Rail Companies Welcome Return to the Office after Commuting Slump', *Independent*, 19 January 2022, https://www.independent.co.uk/travel/ news-and-advice/public-transport-working-commuters-train-b1996441.ht ml (accessed 15 March 2022).

38   Greg Marsden et al., *At a Crossroads*.

39   The concept of the fifteen-minute neighbourhood has been articulated in a number of similar ways. For an overview and discussion see Carlos Moreno et al., 'Introducing the "15-Minute City": Sustainability, Resilience and Place Identity in Future Post-Pandemic Cities', *Smart Cities* 4, no. 1 (2021): 93–111, doi: 10.3390/smartcities4010006.

40   Chris Giles, 'Sunak Faces the Brutal Maths of Electric Vehicles', *Financial Times*, 30 September 2021, https://www.ft.com/content/9f498c0c-4668-47ca-8874-a327e6f11aeb (accessed 15 March 2022).

41   Chris Rosamond, 'UK Road Pricing Plans: Other Solutions to the Fuel Duty "Black Hole" are Available', 16 February 2022, https://www.autoex press.co.uk/news/108123/uk-road-pricing-plans-other-solutions-fuel-duty-black-hole-are-available (accessed 15 March 2022).

42   The reallocation of road space using temporary materials in cities such as Paris and London showed just how quickly (and cheaply) this can be achieved. See Nicolò Fenu, 'Bicycle and Urban Design: A Lesson from Covid-19', *TeMA: Journal of Land Use, Mobility and Environment* 14, no. 1 (2021): 69–92, doi: 10.6092/1970-9870/7716; James O'Malley, 'On Yer Bike: Since Covid-19 First Hit, London has Almost Doubled the Amount of Segregated Cycling Infrastructure and Created Dozens of "Low Traffic Neighbourhoods"', *Engineering & Technology* 16, no. 3 (2021): 52–55, doi: 10.1049/et.2021.0328.

43   Stefan Gössling and Andreas Humpe, 'The Global Scale, Distribution and Growth of Aviation: Implications for Climate Change', *Global Environmental Change* 65 (2020), doi: 10.1016/j.gloenvcha.2020.102194.

44   Tone Smith, ed., *Degrowth of Aviation: Reducing Air Travel in a Just Way* (Stay Grounded/Kollektiv Periskop, December 2019), https://stay-grounded.org/wp-content/uploads/2020/02/Degrowth-Of-Aviation_201 9.pdf (accessed 15 March 2022).

45 Transform Scotland, *A Green Journey to Growth* (Transform Scotland, n.d.), https://transform.scot/wp/wp-content/uploads/2017/08/A-Green-Journey-to-Growth-Transform-Scotland-report.pdf (accessed 15 March 2022).

46 Of course, this would mean increased use of the Channel Tunnel, as well as ferry services, some of which would need to be restored, having been cut in recent years. Although ferries are far from carbon-neutral, they are far more carbon-efficient than planes. However, carbon-neutral shipping is possibly the most difficult of all the transport conundrums posed by a just transition. It is problem that must be overcome, although it is far beyond the scope of this book.

47 Although the technology needs to develop and scale up.

48 For example, money is saved on collecting and enforcing fares, and the economic value created by free public transport be successfully recouped by local taxes. See Wojciech Kębłowski, 'Why (Not) Abolish Fares? Exploring the Global Geography of Fare-Free Public Transport, *Transportation* 47, no. 6 (2020): 2807–2835, doi: 10.1007/s11116-019-09986-6.

49 Office of Rail and Road, *Rail Infrastructure and Assets 2019–20* (Office of Rail and Road, 5 November 2020), https://dataportal.orr.gov.uk/media/1842/rail-infrastructure-assets-2019-20.pdf (accessed 15 March 2022).

50 National Audit Office, *Investigation into the Department for Transport's Decision to Cancel Three Rail Electrification Projects* (National Audit Office, 29 March 2018), https://www.nao.org.uk/wp-content/uploads/2018/03/Investigation-into-the-Department-for-Transports-decision-to-cancel-thr ee-rail-electrification-projects.pdf (accessed 15 March 2022).

51 Author's calculations, based on data from Office of Rail and Road statistics, Table 6320. See 'Welcome to the ORR Data Portal', Office of Rail and Road. 13,000 kilometres represent 82 per cent of the current network. The remaining 18 per cent of lines are lightly used. It is possible that batteries could power trains on these lines, although the technology has not yet been successfully used at scale, and the railways would be competing with the global automotive sector for the battery supply, which will become scarce.

52 Devanjana Nag, 'Indian Railways Green Target: Check Out the Progress Made on 100% Electrification Mission', 18 January 2022, https://www.financialexpress.com/infrastructure/railways/indian-railways-green-targe t-check-out-the-progress-made-on-100-electrification-mission/2409268/ (accessed 15 March 2022).

53 This was the promise of the Theresa May-led Conservative government, and was later adopted by Boris Johnson's government. However, the £500 million allocated to line reopenings as part of the Restoring Your Railway Fund is modest, and certainly does not tally with the bellicose rhetoric surrounding the announcements. For example, restoration of services to Okehampton in Devon – the only project so far to be completed – cost central government £40 million, or 8 per cent of the entire fund, and this was really a project to upgrade an existing route, so it did not bear the full costs of reopening. Despite an impressive list of expressions of interest from around the country for openings, £500 million will not buy much. See 'Restoring your Railway Fund', Department for Transport, 27 October 2021, https://www.gov.uk/government/publications/re-opening-beeching-era-lines-and-stations/re-opening-beeching-era-lines-and-statio ns (accessed 15 March 2022).

54 Greg Marsden, Kadambari Lokesh and Danielle Densley-Tingley, *Everything Counts: Why Transport Infrastructure Emissions Matter for Decision Makers* (DecarboN8, February 2022), https://decarbon8.org.uk/wp-content/uploads/sites/59/2022/02/Everything-Counts-Why-transpor t-infrastructure-emissions-matter-for-decision-makers.pdf (accessed 15 March 2022).

55 Patrick Barkham, 'Will HS2 Really Help Cut the UK's Carbon Footprint?', *Guardian*, 2 February 2020, https://www.theguardian.com/uk-news/2020/feb/02/will-hs2-really-help-cut-the-uks-carbon-footprint#: ~:text=The%20government's%20own%20calculations%20for,will%20not %20cut%20carbon%20emissions (accessed 15 March 2022).

56 David Law, 'Is a Zero-Carbon Skyscraper Possible?', *CTBUH Journal* 3 (2021): 28–34, https://global.ctbuh.org/resources/papers/download/4494-is-a-zero-carbon-concrete-skyscraper-possible.pdf (accessed 15 March 2022).

57 See, for example, Madeline Grant, 'HS2 is a Classic Case of the "Sunk Costs" Fallacy', *Institute of Economic Affairs Blog*, 9 August 2018, https://iea.org.uk/hs2-is-a-classic-case-of-the-sunk-costs-fallacy (accessed 15 March 2022). See also Douglas Oakervee, *Oakervee Review* (HM Government, December 2019), https://assets.publishing.service.gov.uk/government/uploads/system/uploads/attachment_data/file/870092/oakervee-review.pdf (accessed 15 March 2022).

58 Railfuture has published some engaging proposals of what a 'net-zero' approach to capacity improvements could look like, which correctly take the challenge of electrification and bottleneck alleviation together. See Ian

Brown and Chris Page, 'Electrification Mix', Railfuture, 28 July 2020, https://www.railfuture.org.uk/article1862-Electrification-mix (accessed 15 March 2022).

59 Suggestions are inspired by those proposed by the Campaign for Better Transport. See 'Re-opening Rail Lines', Campaign for Better Transport, https://bettertransport.org.uk/re-opening-rail-lines (accessed 19 March 2022). There are also places without railway stations where connections to light rail or metro networks may be more appropriate, such as Washington in Tyne and Wear and Rawtenstall in Lancashire. This list also disregards the possibility of new freight-only lines. A decision on what new freight-only lines are needed depends on how the provision of goods and materials change under a just transition. A just transition will mean the decline of some industries and the rise of others. To a limited extent, these shifts are already occurring. The British rail system's income was once heavily dependent on coal traffic, but, thanks to the relative decarbonisation of power generation, this has declined to almost nothing, meaning the closure or mothballing of many lines.

60 See 'Manchester and East Midlands Rail Action Partnership Limited', MEMRAP, https://www.memrap.org/ (accessed 19 March 2022).

61 See AECOM, *Leicester–Burton Rail Passenger Service Final Report* (Leicestershire County Council, Leicester City Council and North West Leicestershire District Council, May 2016), https://www.nwleics.gov.uk/files/documents/leicester_to_burton_study/Leicester%20-%20Burton%20Rail%20Passenger%20Service_FINAL%20Report_.pdf (accessed 15 March 2022).

62 See 'Manchester to Sheffield Road Tunnel Could be Dropped', *BBC News*, 25 January 2021, https://www.bbc.co.uk/news/uk-england-south-yorkshire-55797936 (accessed 15 March 2022). National Grid's decision to use one of the Woodhead tunnels for power lines does complicate matters. It could be that the older tunnels could be re-activated, but that would depend on survey work. See Ray King, 'Woodhead Spurned', *Railfuture*, 7 March 2018, https://railfuture.org.uk/article1774-Woodhead-spurned (accessed 15 March 2022).

63 'The Okehampton Line', Railfuture, https://www.railfuture.org.uk/The-Okehampton-Line (accessed 19 March 2022); David Dawson, Jon Shaw and W. Roland Gehrels, 'Sea-Level Rise Impacts on Transport Infrastructure: The Notorious Case of the Coastal Railway Line at Dawlish, England', *Journal of Transport Geography* 51 (2016): 97–109, doi: 10.1016/j.jtrangeo.2015.11.009.

64 Neil Pooran, 'Petition to Reopen Stations on Edinburgh's Long-Lost "Circle Line"', *Edinburgh Live*, 2 March 2020, https://www.edinburghli ve.co.uk/news/edinburgh-news/petition-reopen-stations-edinburghs-long -17846800 (accessed 15 March 2022).

65 It would form part of a larger 'West Midlands Metro' plan, which is promoted by Andy Street, the mayor of the West Midlands, but has not yet received funding. See 'Andy Street's £15 Billion Transport Plan Includes Metro Routes for Sutton and Reopening the Park Railway Line', Andy Street, 14 February 2020, https://www.andystreet.org.uk/news/ andy-streets-ps15-billion-transport-plan-includes-metro-routes-sutton-an d-reopening-park#:~:text=Under%20the%20plans%2C%20The%20Sutto n,new%20Moore%20Street%20HS2%20station (accessed 15 March 2022).

66 It would be sensible if this could form an extension to the Merseyrail network. See 'A Station Back in Skelmersdale', Railfuture, https://www. railfuture.org.uk/A+Station+Back+in+Skelmersdale (accessed 19 March 2022).

67 Indeed, the ridiculousness of the situation was starting to change government thinking on the importance of maintaining first-class carriages. See Julia Gregory, 'Chris Grayling Calls for End to First-Class Carriages on Commuter Trains', *Guardian*, 22 July 2017, https://www.theguardian.c om/cities/2017/jul/22/chris-grayling-no-more-first-class-carriages-on-com muter-trains (accessed 15 March 2022).

68 These kinds of facility are standard on many European rail networks.

69 According to Network Rail Chief Executive Andrew Haines. Haines, cited in Rodger Ford, 'Informed Sources: Operators Facing Revenue-Cost Gap', *Modern Railways*, March 2022, 22–24.

70 Author's calculations, based on the latest pre-Covid-19 figures from Office of Rail and Road, Table 1212. See 'Welcome to the ORR Data Portal', Office of Rail and Road.

71 Author's calculations, based on Office of Rail and Road, Table 7270. See 'Welcome to the ORR Data Portal', Office of Rail and Road.

72 Jacob Lewis, 'Greggs Bacon Rolls and Mindfulness Apps Offered to Train Commuters in a Bid to Lure Them Back onto the Railway', *inews*, 27 January 2022, https://inews.co.uk/inews-lifestyle/travel/greggs-bacon-rolls-mindfulness-apps-train-commuters-lure-back-railway-1423934 (accessed 15 March 2022).

73 Car occupancy rates in England from Department for Transport statistics Table NTS0905. See 'Vehicle Mileage and Occupancy', Department for Transport, 22 September 2021, https://www.gov.uk/government/

statistical-data-sets/nts09-vehicle-mileage-and-occupancy (accessed 15 March 2022). Motoring costs taken from Erin Yurday, 'Average Cost to Run a Car UK 2022', NimbleFins, 12 November 2021, https://www. nimblefins.co.uk/cheap-car-insurance/average-cost-run-car-uk (accessed 15 March 2022).

74 In the long term it may be possible to de-commodify transport altogether. However, it is difficult to see how that could be achieved in a capitalist system. To be sure, non-commodified public services have existed under capitalism, in situations where resources and services are directed at those with the greatest need, not those with the fattest wallets. But transport is very different from, for example, nationalised health services. There, service experts – for example doctors – can make case-by-case judgements on patients' needs and allocate care according to its availability. There is no equivalent in transport. Deciding where we go and how we get there is very much a personal choice, albeit one constrained by the demands of our lives and the availability of transport options. It is difficult to see how an expert could tell us which journeys are necessary and which are not. On the other hand, the creation of personal transport carbon budgets seems problematic, because it suggests that transport emissions can be reduced through personal choice alone, ignoring the fact that transport is a means to various social ends, not an isolated area of personal consumption. A much more holistic approach is required, involving a thorough and critical appreciation of the political economy of how we make things and consume them, the social relations of work and sexual and social reproduction, how we care for each other, and how those aspects of our lives will need to change in order to remain within carbon budgets while reducing inequalities. Only by aligning with such work can we truly design transport policy that will enable a just transition.

75 Lewis Harper, 'At 6% of Flights, Long-Haul Services Emit 51% of CO_2: Eurocontrol', *FlightGlobal*, 16 February 2021, https://www.flightglobal. com/networks/at-6-of-flights-long-haul-services-emit-51-of-co2-eurocontr ol/142445.article (accessed 15 March 2022).

76 Adam Graham, 'European Sleeper Trains Make a Comeback', *Wall Street Journal*, 25 August 2021, https://www.wsj.com/articles/european-sleeper-train-climate-change-11629832201 (accessed 15 March 2022).

77 Adrian Vaughan, *Railway Blunders* (Ian Allan, 2003), 133–135.

78 'The Best Time to Prevent the Next Pandemic is Now: Countries Join Voices for Better Emergency Preparedness', World Health Organisation, 1 October 2020, https://www.who.int/news/item/01-10-20

20-the-best-time-to-prevent-the-next-pandemic-is-now-countries-join-vo ices-for-better-emergency-preparedness (accessed 15 March 2022); Gregory Gray, Emily Robie, Caleb Studstill and Charles Nunn, 'Mitigating Future Respiratory Virus Pandemics: New Threats and Approaches to Consider', *Viruses* 13, no. 4 (2021): 637, doi: 10.3390/v13040637.

79 European Union Agency for Railways, *Covid-19 Information Bulletin: Ventilation in Railway Vehicles* (European Union Agency for Railways, September 2020), https://www.era.europa.eu/sites/default/files/ events-news/docs/covid-19_bulletin_ventilation_in_railway_vehicles_en. pdf (accessed 15 March 2022).

80 Indeed, a briefing by the Rail Delivery Group seems to try to put the matter to rest by stating that 'The EU Agency for Railways has stated that ventilation systems on trains, which renew the air in a carriage at least every ten minutes, are important to extract harmful aerosols including coronavirus, suggesting that trains may be safer than some other indoor settings' ('Rail Companies Add Services so People can Travel with Confidence as Britain Steps out of Lockdown', Rail Delivery Group, 8 April 2021, https://media. raildeliverygroup.com/news/rail-companies-add-services-so-people-can-travel-with-confidence-as-britain-steps-out-of-lockdown (accessed 15 March 2022)). In fact, the agency's report goes on to outline a series of measures that operators could take to increase ventilation in air-conditioned rolling stock. See European Union Agency for Railways, *Covid-19 Information Bulletin*. The present author could not find any evidence of those measures, including the relatively simple one of automatic door opening at stations, having been introduced on British rolling stock.

81 Driving can be disincentivised in other ways, such as reallocating road space from cars to buses, pedestrians and cyclists, and reducing car parking facilities.

82 More will be needed for the proposed infrastructure expansions, which could be funded by public borrowing.

83 Jeffery, 'Why We Need to Act', 9.

84 'How has Inequality Changed?', Equality Trust, https://equalitytrust.org. uk/how-has-inequality-changed (accessed 19 March 2022).

85 'Distribution of Individual Total Wealth by Characteristic in Great Britain: April 2018 to March 2020' Office for National Statistics, 7 January 2022, https://www.ons.gov.uk/peoplepopulationandcommunity/personalandh ouseholdfinances/incomeandwealth/bulletins/distributionofindividualtot alwealthbycharacteristicingreatbritain/april2018tomarch2020 (accessed 15 March 2022).

86 Arun Advani, Emma Chamberlain and Andy Summers, *A Wealth Tax for the UK* (Wealth Tax Commission, 9 December 2020), https://www.ukwealth.tax/ (accessed 15 March 2022).

87 Jon Stone and Andrew Woodcock, 'Budget: Rishi Sunak Makes Flights Cheaper Despite Warnings to Cut UK's Air-Travel Demand', *Independent*, 27 October 2021, https://www.independent.co.uk/climate-change/news/budget-flight-tax-cut-cop26-b1946258.html (accessed 15 March 2022).

88 Jim Pickard, Philip Georgiadis and Gill Plimmer, 'Johnson Backs Cut in Air Passenger Duty to Aid UK Domestic Flights', *Financial Times*, 9 March 2021, https://www.ft.com/content/70bbc71d-50f5-49fd-97d3-36625146e7d9 (accessed 15 March 2022). Hendy dismisses concerns that subsidising domestic air travel will hurt decarbonisation efforts by making a familiar appeal to unproved 'alternative fuels'. See Peter Hendy, *Union Connectivity Review: Final Report* (Department for Transport, November 2021), https://assets.publishing.service.gov.uk/government/uploads/system/uploads/attachment_data/file/1036027/union-connectivity-review-final-report.pdf (accessed 15 March 2022).

89 Hendy, *Union Connectivity Review*, 11.

90 Lisa Hopkinson and Lynn Sloman, *Getting the Department for Transport on the Right Track: A Damning Indictment of the Failure of the Department for Transport to Give Proper Regard to the Climate Change Act* (Friends of the Earth, May 2019), https://policy.friendsoftheearth.uk/print/pdf/node/108 (accessed 15 March 2022).

91 Naomi Klein, *This Changes Everything: Capitalism vs. the Climate* (Simon and Schuster, 2015).

92 Cox and Nilsen call issue-specific campaigns 'militant particularisms'. Laurence Cox and Alf Gunvald Nilsen, *We Make our Own History: Marxism and Social Movements in the Twilight of Neoliberalism* (Pluto Press, 2014), 76.

Index